D0193908

A STREETCAR
NAMED DESIRE

Tennessee Williams

EDITORIAL DIRECTOR Laurie Barnett
DIRECTOR OF TECHNOLOGY Tammy Hepps

SERIES EDITOR John Crowther
MANAGING EDITOR Vince Janoski

WRITERS Jesse Lichtenstein, Deirdre O'Dwyer
EDITORS Jane Carr, Sarah Friedberg

Copyright © 2003 by SparkNotes LLC

All rights reserved. No part of this book may be used or reproduced in any manner
whatsoever without the written permission of the Publisher.

SPARKNOTES is a registered trademark of SparkNotes LLC

This edition published by Spark Publishing

Spark Publishing
A Division of SparkNotes LLC
120 Fifth Avenue, 8th Floor
New York, NY 10011

Any book purchased without a cover is stolen property, reported as "unsold and
destroyed" to the Publisher, who receives no payment for such "stripped books."

Please submit all comments and questions or report errors to www.sparknotes.com/errors

Printed and bound in the United States

ISBN 1-58663-449-6

INTRODUCTION: STOPPING TO BUY SPARKNOTES ON A SNOWY EVENING ·

Whose words these are you *think* you know.
Your paper's due tomorrow, though;
We're glad to see you stopping here
To get some help before you go.

Lost your course? You'll find it here.
Face tests and essays without fear.
Between the words, good grades at stake:
Get great results throughout the year.

Once school bells caused your heart to quake
As teachers circled each mistake.
Use SparkNotes and no longer weep,
Ace every single test you take.

Yes, books are lovely, dark, and deep,
But only what you grasp you keep,
With hours to go before you sleep,
With hours to go before you sleep.

Contents

Context

ENNESSEE WILLIAMS WAS BORN Thomas Lanier Williams III in Columbus, Mississippi, in 1911. His friends began calling him Tennessee in college, in honor of his Southern accent and his father's home state. Williams's father, C.C. Williams, was a traveling salesman and a heavy drinker. Williams's mother, Edwina, was a Mississippi clergyman's daughter prone to hysterical attacks. Until Williams was seven, he, his parents, his older sister, Rose, and his younger brother, Dakin, lived with Edwina's parents in Mississippi.

In 1918, the Williams family moved to St. Louis, marking the start of the family's deterioration. C.C.'s drinking increased, the family moved sixteen times in ten years, and the young Williams, always shy and fragile, was ostracized and taunted at school. During these years, he and Rose became extremely close. Edwina and Williams's maternal grandparents also offered the emotional support he required throughout his childhood. Williams loathed his father but grew to appreciate him somewhat after deciding in therapy as an adult that his father had given him his tough survival instinct.

After being bedridden for two years as a child due to severe illness, Williams grew into a withdrawn, effeminate adolescent whose chief solace was writing. At sixteen, Williams won a prize in a national competition that asked for essays answering the question "Can a good wife be a good sport?" His answer was published in *Smart Set* magazine. The following year, he published a horror story in a magazine called *Weird Tales,* and the year after that he entered the University of Missouri to study journalism. While in college, he wrote his first plays, which were influenced by members of the southern literary renaissance such as Robert Penn Warren, William Faulkner, Allen Tate, and Thomas Wolfe. Before Williams could receive his degree, however, his father forced him to withdraw from school. Outraged because Williams had failed a required ROTC program course, C.C. Williams made his son go to work at the same shoe company where he himself worked.

After three years at the shoe factory, Williams had a minor nervous breakdown. He then returned to college, this time at Washington University in St. Louis. While he was studying there, a St. Louis theater group produced two of his plays, *The Fugitive Kind* and

CONTEXT

I

Candles to the Sun. Further personal problems led Williams to drop out of Washington University and enroll in the University of Iowa. While he was in Iowa, Rose, who had begun suffering from mental illness later in life, underwent a prefrontal lobotomy (an intensive brain surgery). The event greatly upset Williams, and it left his sister institutionalized for the rest of her life. Despite this trauma, Williams finally managed to graduate in 1938.

In the years following his graduation, Williams lived a bohemian life, working menial jobs and wandering from city to city. He continued to work on drama, however, receiving a Rockefeller grant and studying playwriting at the New School in New York. His literary influences were evolving to include the playwright Anton Chekhov and Williams's lifelong hero, the poet Hart Crane. He officially changed his name to Tennessee Williams upon the publication of his short story "The Field of Blue Children" in 1939. During the early years of World War II, Williams worked in Hollywood as a scriptwriter and also prepared material for what would become *The Glass Menagerie.*

In 1944, *The Glass Menagerie* opened in New York and won the prestigious New York Drama Critics' Circle Award, catapulting Williams into the upper echelon of American playwrights. *A Streetcar Named Desire* premiered three years later at the Barrymore Theater in New York City. The play, set in contemporary times, describes the decline and fall of a fading Southern belle named Blanche DuBois. *A Streetcar Named Desire* cemented Williams's reputation, garnering another Drama Critics' Circle Award and also a Pulitzer Prize. Williams went on to win another Drama Critics' Circle Award and Pulitzer for *Cat on a Hot Tin Roof* in 1955.

Much of the pathos found in Williams's drama was mined from the playwright's own life. Alcoholism, depression, thwarted desire, loneliness, and insanity were all part of Williams's world. His experience as a known homosexual in an era unfriendly to homosexuality also informed his work. Williams's most memorable characters, many of them female, contain recognizable elements of their author, Edwina, and Rose. His vulgar, irresponsible male characters, such as Stanley Kowalski, were likely modeled on Williams's own father and other males who tormented Williams during his childhood.

Williams's early plays also connected with the new American taste for realism that emerged following the Depression and World War II. The characters in *A Streetcar Named Desire* are trying to rebuild their lives in postwar America: Stanley and Mitch served in the military, while Blanche had affairs with young soldiers based near her home.

Williams set his plays in the South, but the compelling manner in which he rendered his themes made them universal, winning him an international audience and worldwide acclaim. However, most critics agree that the quality of Williams's work diminished as he grew older. He suffered a long period of depression following the death of his longtime partner, Frank Merlo, in 1963. His popularity during these years also declined due to changed interests in the theater world. During the radical 1960s and 1970s, nostalgia no longer drew crowds, and Williams's explorations of sexual mores came across as tired and old-fashioned.

Williams died in 1983 when he choked on a medicine-bottle cap in an alcohol-related incident at the Elysée Hotel in New York City. He was one month short of his seventy-second birthday. In his long career he wrote twenty-five full-length plays (five made into movies), five screenplays, over seventy one-act plays, hundreds of short stories, two novels, poetry, and a memoir. The mark he left on the tradition of realism in American drama is indelible.

A NOTE ON THE EPIGRAPH

The epigraph to *A Streecar Named Desire* is taken from a Hart Crane poem titled "The Broken Tower." Crane was one of Williams's icons. Williams's use of this quotation is apt, as Crane himself often employed epigraphs from his own icons, including Melville, Whitman, Dickinson, and Blake. Williams felt a personal affinity with Crane, who, like himself, had a bitter relationship with his parents and suffered from bouts of violent alcoholism. Most important, Williams identified with Crane as a homosexual writer trying to find a means of self-expression in a heterosexual world. Unlike Williams, Crane succumbed to his demons, drowning himself in 1932 at the age of thirty-three.

Williams was influenced by Crane's imagery and by his unusual attention to metaphor. The epigraph's description of love as only an "instant" and as a force that precipitates "each desperate choice" brings to mind Williams's character Blanche DuBois. Crane's speaker's line, "I know not whither [love's voice is] hurled," also suggests Blanche. With increasing desperation, Blanche "hurls" her continually denied love out into the world, only to have that love revisit her in the form of suffering.

PLOT OVERVIEW

BLANCHE DUBOIS, A SCHOOLTEACHER from Laurel, Mississippi, arrives at the New Orleans apartment of her sister, Stella Kowalski. Despite the fact that Blanche seems to have fallen out of close contact with Stella, she intends to stay at Stella's apartment for an unspecified but likely lengthy period of time, given the large trunk she has with her. Blanche tells Stella that she lost Belle Reve, their ancestral home, following the death of all their remaining relatives. She also mentions that she has been given a leave of absence from her teaching position because of her bad nerves.

Though Blanche does not seem to have enough money to afford a hotel, she is disdainful of the cramped quarters of the Kowalskis' two-room apartment and of the apartment's location in a noisy, diverse, working-class neighborhood. Blanche's social condescension wins her the instant dislike of Stella's husband, an auto-parts supply man of Polish descent named Stanley Kowalski. It is clear that Stella was happy to leave behind her the social pretensions of her background in exchange for the sexual gratification she gets from her husband; she even is pregnant with his baby. Stanley immediately distrusts Blanche to the extent that he suspects her of having cheated Stella out of her share of the family inheritance. In the process of defending herself to Stanley, Blanche reveals that Belle Reve was lost due to a foreclosed mortgage, a disclosure that signifies the dire nature of Blanche's financial circumstances. Blanche's heavy drinking, which she attempts to conceal from her sister and brother-in-law, is another sign that all is not well with Blanche.

The unhappiness that accompanies the animal magnetism of Stella and Stanley's marriage reveals itself when Stanley hosts a drunken poker game with his male friends at the apartment. Blanche gets under Stanley's skin, especially when she starts to win the affections of his close friend Mitch. After Mitch has been absent for a while, speaking with Blanche in the bedroom, Stanley erupts, storms into the bedroom, and throws the radio out of the window. When Stella yells at Stanley and defends Blanche, Stanley beats her. The men pull him off, the poker game breaks up, and Blanche and Stella escape to their upstairs neighbor Eunice's apartment. A short while later, Stanley is remorseful and cries up to Stella to forgive him. To Blanche's alarm, Stella returns to Stanley and embraces him passionately. Mitch meets Blanche outside of the Kowalski flat and comforts her in her distress.

The next day, Blanche tries to convince Stella to leave Stanley for a better man whose social status equals Stella's. Blanche suggests that she and Stella contact a millionaire named Shep Huntleigh for help escaping from New Orleans; when Stella laughs at her, Blanche reveals that she is completely broke. Stanley walks in as Blanche is making fun of him and secretly overhears Blanche and Stella's conversation. Later, he threatens Blanche with hints that he has heard rumors of her disreputable past. She is visibly dismayed.

While Blanche is alone in the apartment one evening, waiting for Mitch to pick her up for a date, a teenage boy comes by to collect money for the newspaper. Blanche doesn't have any money for him, but she hits on him and gives him a lustful kiss. Soon after the boy departs, Mitch arrives, and they go on their date. When Blanche returns, she is exhausted and clearly has been uneasy for the entire night about the rumors Stanley mentioned earlier. In a surprisingly sincere heart-to-heart discussion with Mitch, Blanche reveals the greatest tragedy of her past. Years ago, her young husband committed suicide after she discovered and chastised him for his homosexuality. Mitch describes his own loss of a former love, and he tells Blanche that they need each other.

When the next scene begins, about one month has passed. It is the afternoon of Blanche's birthday. Stella is preparing a dinner for Blanche, Mitch, Stanley, and herself, when Stanley comes in to tell her that he has learned news of Blanche's sordid past. He says that after losing the DuBois mansion, Blanche moved into a fleabag motel from which she was eventually evicted because of her numerous sexual liaisons. Also, she was fired from her job as a schoolteacher because the principal discovered that she was having an affair with a teenage student. Stella is horrified to learn that Stanley has told Mitch these stories about Blanche.

The birthday dinner comes and goes, but Mitch never arrives. Stanley indicates to Blanche that he is aware of her past. For a birthday present, he gives her a one-way bus ticket back to Laurel. Stanley's cruelty so disturbs Stella that it appears the Kowalski household is about to break up, but the onset of Stella's labor prevents the imminent fight.

Several hours later, Blanche, drunk, sits alone in the apartment. Mitch, also drunk, arrives and repeats all he's learned from Stanley.

Eventually Blanche confesses that the stories are true, but she also reveals the need for human affection she felt after her husband's death. Mitch tells Blanche that he can never marry her, saying she isn't fit to live in the same house as his mother. Having learned that Blanche is not the chaste lady she pretended to be, Mitch tries to have sex with Blanche, but she forces him to leave by yelling "Fire!" to attract the attention of passersby outside.

Later, Stanley returns from the hospital to find Blanche even more drunk. She tells him that she will soon be leaving New Orleans with her former suitor Shep Huntleigh, who is now a millionaire. Stanley knows that Blanche's story is entirely in her imagination, but he is so happy about his baby that he proposes they each celebrate their good fortune. Blanche spurns Stanley, and things grow contentious. When she tries to step past him, he refuses to move out of her way. Blanche becomes terrified to the point that she smashes a bottle on the table and threatens to smash Stanley in the face. Stanley grabs her arm and says that it's time for the "date" they've had set up since Blanche's arrival. Blanche resists, but Stanley uses his physical strength to overcome her, and he carries her to bed. The pulsing music indicates that Stanley rapes Blanche.

The next scene takes place weeks later, as Stella and her neighbor Eunice pack Blanche's bags. Blanche is in the bath, and Stanley plays poker with his buddies in the front room. A doctor will arrive soon to take Blanche to an insane asylum, but Blanche believes she is leaving to join her millionaire. Stella confesses to Eunice that she simply cannot allow herself to believe Blanche's assertion that Stanley raped her. When Blanche emerges from the bathroom, her deluded talk makes it clear that she has lost her grip on reality.

The doctor arrives with a nurse, and Blanche initially panics and struggles against them when they try to take her away. Stanley and his friends fight to subdue Blanche, while Eunice holds Stella back to keep her from interfering. Mitch begins to cry. Finally, the doctor approaches Blanche in a gentle manner and convinces her to leave with him. She allows him to lead her away and does not look back or say goodbye as she goes. Stella sobs with her child in her arms, and Stanley comforts her with loving words and caresses.

CHARACTER LIST

Blanche DuBois Stella's older sister, who was a high school English teacher in Laurel, Mississippi, until she was forced to leave her post. Blanche is a loquacious and fragile woman around the age of thirty. After losing Belle Reve, the DuBois family home, Blanche arrives in New Orleans at the Kowalski apartment and eventually reveals that she is completely destitute. Though she has strong sexual urges and has had many lovers, she puts on the airs of a woman who has never known indignity. She avoids reality, preferring to live in her own imagination. As the play progresses, Blanche's instability grows along with her misfortune. Stanley sees through Blanche and finds out the details of her past, destroying her relationship with his friend Mitch. Stanley also destroys what's left of Blanche by raping her and then having her committed to an insane asylum.

Stella Kowalski Blanche's younger sister, about twenty-five years old and of a mild disposition that visibly sets her apart from her more vulgar neighbors. Stella possesses the same timeworn aristocratic heritage as Blanche, but she jumped the sinking ship in her late teens and left Mississippi for New Orleans. There, Stella married lower-class Stanley, with whom she shares a robust sexual relationship. Stella's union with Stanley is both animal and spiritual, violent but renewing. After Blanche's arrival, Stella is torn between her sister and her husband. Eventually, she stands by Stanley, perhaps in part because she gives birth to his child near the play's end. While she loves and pities Blanche, she cannot bring herself to believe Blanche's accusations that Stanley dislikes Blanche, and she eventually dismisses Blanche's claim that Stanley raped her. Stella's denial of reality at the play's end shows that she has more in common with her sister than she thinks.

Stanley Kowalski   The husband of Stella. Stanley is the epitome of vital force. He is loyal to his friends, passionate to his wife, and heartlessly cruel to Blanche. With his Polish ancestry, he represents the new, heterogeneous America. He sees himself as a social leveler, and wishes to destroy Blanche's social pretensions. Around thirty years of age, Stanley, who fought in World War II, now works as an auto-parts salesman. Practicality is his forte, and he has no patience for Blanche's distortions of the truth. He lacks ideals and imagination. By the play's end, he is a disturbing degenerate: he beats his wife and rapes his sister-in-law. Horrifyingly, he shows no remorse. Yet, Blanche is an outcast from society, while Stanley is the proud family man.

Harold "Mitch" Mitchell   Stanley's army friend, coworker, and poker buddy, who courts Blanche until he finds out that she lied to him about her sordid past. Mitch, like Stanley, is around thirty years of age. Though he is clumsy, sweaty, and has unrefined interests like muscle building, Mitch is more sensitive and more gentlemanly than Stanley and his other friends, perhaps because he lives with his mother, who is slowly dying. Blanche and Mitch are an unlikely match: Mitch doesn't fit the bill of the chivalric hero, the man Blanche dreams will come to rescue her. Nevertheless, they bond over their lost loves, and when the doctor takes Blanche away against her will, Mitch is the only person present besides Stella who despairs over the tragedy.

Eunice   Stella's friend, upstairs neighbor, and landlady. Eunice and her husband, Steve, represent the low-class, carnal life that Stella has chosen for herself. Like Stella, Eunice accepts her husband's affections despite his physical abuse of her. At the end of the play, when Stella hesitates to stay with Stanley at Blanche's expense, Eunice forbids Stella to question her decision and tells her she has no choice but to disbelieve Blanche.

Allan Grey The young man with poetic aspirations whom Blanche fell in love with and married as a teenager. One afternoon, she discovered Allan in bed with an older male friend. That evening at a ball, after she announced her disgust at his homosexuality, he ran outside and shot himself in the head. Allan's death, which marked the end of Blanche's sexual innocence, has haunted her ever since. Long dead by the time of the play's action, Allan never appears onstage.

A Young Collector A teenager who comes to the Kowalskis' door to collect for the newspaper when Blanche is home alone. The boy leaves bewildered after Blanche hits on him and gives him a passionate farewell kiss. He embodies Blanche's obsession with youth and presumably reminds her of her teenage love, the young poet Allan Grey, whom she married and lost to suicide. Blanche's flirtation with the newspaper collector also displays her unhealthy sexual preoccupation with teenage boys, which we learn of later in the play.

Shep Huntleigh A former suitor of Blanche's whom she met again a year before her arrival in New Orleans while vacationing in Miami. Despite the fact that Shep is married, Blanche hopes he will provide the financial support for her and Stella to escape from Stanley. As Blanche's mental stability deteriorates, her fantasy that Shep is coming to sweep her away becomes more and more real to her. Shep never appears onstage.

Steve Stanley's poker buddy who lives upstairs with his wife, Eunice. Like Stanley, Steve is a brutish, hot-blooded, physically fit male and an abusive husband.

Pablo Stanley's poker buddy. Like Stanley and Steve, Steve is physically fit and brutish. Pablo is Hispanic, and his friendship with Steve, Stanley, and Mitch emphasizes the culturally diverse nature of their neighborhood.

CHARACTER LIST

A Negro Woman In Scene One, the Negro woman is sitting on the steps talking to Eunice when Blanche arrives, and she finds Stanley's openly sexual gestures toward Stella hilarious. Later, in Scene Ten, we see her scurrying across the stage in the night as she rifles through a prostitute's lost handbag.

A Doctor At the play's finale, the doctor arrives to whisk Blanche off to an asylum. He and the nurse initially seem to be heartless institutional caretakers, but, in the end, the doctor appears more kindly as he takes off his jacket and leads Blanche away. This image of the doctor ironically conforms to Blanche's notions of the chivalric Southern gentleman who will offer her salvation.

A Mexican Woman A vendor of Mexican funeral decorations who frightens Blanche by issuing the plaintive call "*Flores para los muertos,*" which means "Flowers for the dead."

A Nurse Also called the "Matron," she accompanies the doctor to collect Blanche and bring her to an institution. She possesses a severe, unfeminine manner and has a talent for subduing hysterical patients.

Shaw A supply man who is Stanley's coworker and his source for stories of Blanche's disreputable past in Laurel, Mississippi. Shaw travels regularly through Laurel.

Prostitute Moments before Stanley rapes Blanche, the back wall of the Kowalskis' apartment becomes transparent, and Blanche sees a prostitute in the street being pursued by a male drunkard. The prostitute's situation evokes Blanche's own predicament. After the prostitute and the drunkard pass, the Negro woman scurries by with the prostitute's lost handbag in hand.

ANALYSIS OF MAJOR CHARACTERS

BLANCHE DuBOIS

When the play begins, Blanche is already a fallen woman in society's eyes. Her family fortune and estate are gone, she lost her young husband to suicide years earlier, and she is a social pariah due to her indiscrete sexual behavior. She also has a bad drinking problem, which she covers up poorly. Behind her veneer of social snobbery and sexual propriety, Blanche is an insecure, dislocated individual. She is an aging Southern belle who lives in a state of perpetual panic about her fading beauty. Her manner is dainty and frail, and she sports a wardrobe of showy but cheap evening clothes. Stanley quickly sees through Blanche's act and seeks out information about her past.

In the Kowalski household, Blanche pretends to be a woman who has never known indignity. Her false propriety is not simply snobbery, however; it constitutes a calculated attempt to make herself appear attractive to new male suitors. Blanche depends on male sexual admiration for her sense of self-esteem, which means that she has often succumbed to passion. By marrying, Blanche hopes to escape poverty and the bad reputation that haunts her. But because the chivalric Southern gentleman savior and caretaker (represented by Shep Huntleigh) she hopes will rescue her is extinct, Blanche is left with no realistic possibility of future happiness. As Blanche sees it, Mitch is her only chance for contentment, even though he is far from her ideal.

Stanley's relentless persecution of Blanche foils her pursuit of Mitch as well as her attempts to shield herself from the harsh truth of her situation. The play chronicles the subsequent crumbling of Blanche's self-image and sanity. Stanley himself takes the final stabs at Blanche, destroying the remainder of her sexual and mental esteem by raping her and then committing her to an insane asylum. In the end, Blanche blindly allows herself to be led away by a kind doctor, ignoring her sister's cries. This final image is the sad culmination of Blanche's vanity and total dependence upon men for happiness.

STANLEY KOWALSKI

Audience members may well see Stanley as an egalitarian hero at the play's start. He is loyal to his friends and passionate to his wife. Stanley possesses an animalistic physical vigor that is evident in his love of work, of fighting, and of sex. His family is from Poland, and several times he expresses his outrage at being called "Polack" and other derogatory names. When Blanche calls him a "Polack," he makes her look old-fashioned and ignorant by asserting that he was born in America, is an American, and can only be called "Polish." Stanley represents the new, heterogeneous America to which Blanche doesn't belong, because she is a relic from a defunct social hierarchy. He sees himself as a social leveler, as he tells Stella in Scene Eight.

Stanley's intense hatred of Blanche is motivated in part by the aristocratic past Blanche represents. He also (rightly) sees her as untrustworthy and does not appreciate the way she attempts to fool him and his friends into thinking she is better than they are. Stanley's animosity toward Blanche manifests itself in all of his actions toward her—his investigations of her past, his birthday gift to her, his sabotage of her relationship with Mitch.

In the end, Stanley's down-to-earth character proves harmfully crude and brutish. His chief amusements are gambling, bowling, sex, and drinking, and he lacks ideals and imagination. His disturbing, degenerate nature, first hinted at when he beats his wife, is fully evident after he rapes his sister-in-law. Stanley shows no remorse for his brutal actions. The play ends with an image of Stanley as the ideal family man, comforting his wife as she holds their newborn child. The wrongfulness of this representation, given what we have learned about him in the play, ironically calls into question society's decision to ostracize Blanche.

HAROLD "MITCH" MITCHELL

Perhaps because he lives with his dying mother, Mitch is noticeably more sensitive than Stanley's other poker friends. The other men pick on him for being a mama's boy. Even in his first, brief line in Scene One, Mitch's gentlemanly behavior stands out. Mitch appears to be a kind, decent human being who, we learn in Scene Six, hopes to marry so that he will have a woman to bring home to his dying mother.

Mitch doesn't fit the bill of the chivalric hero of whom Blanche dreams. He is clumsy, sweaty, and has unrefined interests like muscle building. Though sensitive, he lacks Blanche's romantic perspective and spirituality, as well as her understanding of poetry and literature. She toys with his lack of intelligence—for example, when she teases him in French because she knows he won't understand—duping him into playing along with her self-flattering charades.

Though they come from completely different worlds, Mitch and Blanche are drawn together by their mutual need of companionship and support, and they therefore believe themselves right for one another. They also discover that they have both experienced the death of a loved one. The snare in their relationship is sexual. As part of her prim-and-proper act, Blanche repeatedly rejects Mitch's physical affections, refusing to sleep with him. Once he discovers the truth about Blanche's sordid sexual past, Mitch is both angry and embarrassed about the way Blanche has treated him. When he arrives to chastise her, he states that he feels he deserves to have sex with her, even though he no longer respects her enough to think her fit to be his wife.

The difference in Stanley's and Mitch's treatment of Blanche at the play's end underscores Mitch's fundamental gentlemanliness. Though he desires and makes clear that he wants to sleep with Blanche, Mitch does not rape her and leaves when she cries out. Also, the tears Mitch sheds after Blanche struggles to escape the fate Stanley has arranged for her show that he genuinely cares for her. In fact, Mitch is the only person other than Stella who seems to understand the tragedy of Blanche's madness.

CHARACTER ANALYSIS

THEMES, MOTIFS & SYMBOLS

THEMES

Themes are the fundamental and often universal ideas explored in a literary work.

FANTASY'S INABILITY TO OVERCOME REALITY

Although Williams's protagonist in *A Streetcar Named Desire* is the romantic Blanche DuBois, the play is a work of social realism. Blanche explains to Mitch that she fibs because she refuses to accept the hand fate has dealt her. Lying to herself and to others allows her to make life appear as it should be rather than as it is. Stanley, a practical man firmly grounded in the physical world, disdains Blanche's fabrications and does everything he can to unravel them. The antagonistic relationship between Blanche and Stanley is a struggle between appearances and reality. It propels the play's plot and creates an overarching tension. Ultimately, Blanche's attempts to remake her own and Stella's existences—to rejuvenate her life and to save Stella from a life with Stanley—fail.

One of the main ways Williams dramatizes fantasy's inability to overcome reality is through an exploration of the boundary between exterior and interior. The set of the play consists of the two-room Kowalski apartment and the surrounding street. Williams's use of a flexible set that allows the street to be seen at the same time as the interior of the home expresses the notion that the home is not a domestic sanctuary. The Kowalskis' apartment cannot be a self-defined world that is impermeable to greater reality. The characters leave and enter the apartment throughout the play, often bringing with them the problems they encounter in the larger environment. For example, Blanche refuses to leave her prejudices against the working class behind her at the door. The most notable instance of this effect occurs just before Stanley rapes Blanche, when the back wall of the apartment becomes transparent to show the struggles occurring on the street, foreshadowing the violation that is about to take place in the Kowalskis' home.

Though reality triumphs over fantasy in *A Streetcar Named Desire*, Williams suggests that fantasy is an important and useful tool. At the end of the play, Blanche's retreat into her own private fantasies enables her to partially shield herself from reality's harsh blows. Blanche's insanity emerges as she retreats fully into herself, leaving the objective world behind in order to avoid accepting reality. In order to escape fully, however, Blanche must come to perceive the exterior world as that which she imagines in her head. Thus, objective reality is not an antidote to Blanche's fantasy world; rather, Blanche adapts the exterior world to fit her delusions. In both the physical and the psychological realms, the boundary between fantasy and reality is permeable. Blanche's final, deluded happiness suggests that, to some extent, fantasy is a vital force at play in every individual's experience, despite reality's inevitable triumph.

THE RELATIONSHIP BETWEEN SEX AND DEATH

Blanche's fear of death manifests itself in her fears of aging and of lost beauty. She refuses to tell anyone her true age or to appear in harsh light that will reveal her faded looks. She seems to believe that by continually asserting her sexuality, especially toward men younger than herself, she will be able to avoid death and return to the world of teenage bliss she experienced before her husband's suicide.

However, beginning in Scene One, Williams suggests that Blanche's sexual history is in fact a cause of her downfall. When she first arrives at the Kowalskis', Blanche says she rode a streetcar named Desire, then transferred to a streetcar named Cemeteries, which brought her to a street named Elysian Fields. This journey, the precursor to the play, allegorically represents the trajectory of Blanche's life. The Elysian Fields are the land of the dead in Greek mythology. Blanche's lifelong pursuit of her sexual desires has led to her eviction from Belle Reve, her ostracism from Laurel, and, at the end of the play, her expulsion from society at large.

Sex leads to death for others Blanche knows as well. Throughout the play, Blanche is haunted by the deaths of her ancestors, which she attributes to their "epic fornications." Her husband's suicide results from her disapproval of his homosexuality. The message is that indulging one's desire in the form of unrestrained promiscuity leads to forced departures and unwanted ends. In Scene Nine, when the Mexican woman appears selling "flowers for the dead," Blanche reacts with horror because the woman announces Blanche's fate. Her fall into madness can be read as the ending brought about by

THEMES

her dual flaws—her inability to act appropriately on her desire and her desperate fear of human mortality. Sex and death are intricately and fatally linked in Blanche's experience.

DEPENDENCE ON MEN

A Streetcar Named Desire presents a sharp critique of the way the institutions and attitudes of postwar America placed restrictions on women's lives. Williams uses Blanche's and Stella's dependence on men to expose and critique the treatment of women during the transition from the old to the new South. Both Blanche and Stella see male companions as their only means to achieve happiness, and they depend on men for both their sustenance and their self-image. Blanche recognizes that Stella could be happier without her physically abusive husband, Stanley. Yet, the alternative Blanche proposes—contacting Shep Huntleigh for financial support—still involves complete dependence on men. When Stella chooses to remain with Stanley, she chooses to rely on, love, and believe in a man instead of her sister. Williams does not necessarily criticize Stella—he makes it quite clear that Stanley represents a much more secure future than Blanche does.

For herself, Blanche sees marriage to Mitch as her means of escaping destitution. Men's exploitation of Blanche's sexuality has left her with a poor reputation. This reputation makes Blanche an unattractive marriage prospect, but, because she is destitute, Blanche sees marriage as her only possibility for survival. When Mitch rejects Blanche because of Stanley's gossip about her reputation, Blanche immediately thinks of another man—the millionaire Shep Huntleigh—who might rescue her. Because Blanche cannot see around her dependence on men, she has no realistic conception of how to rescue herself. Blanche does not realize that her dependence on men will lead to her downfall rather than her salvation. By relying on men, Blanche puts her fate in the hands of others.

MOTIFS

Motifs are recurring structures, contrasts, or literary devices that can help to develop and inform the text's major themes.

LIGHT

Throughout the play, Blanche avoids appearing in direct, bright light, especially in front of her suitor, Mitch. She also refuses to reveal her age, and it is clear that she avoids light in order to prevent him from seeing the reality of her fading beauty. In general, light also symbolizes the reality of Blanche's past. She is haunted by the ghosts of what she has lost—her first love, her purpose in life, her dignity, and the genteel society (real or imagined) of her ancestors.

Blanche covers the exposed lightbulb in the Kowalski apartment with a Chinese paper lantern, and she refuses to go on dates with Mitch during the daytime or to well-lit locations. Mitch points out Blanche's avoidance of light in Scene Nine, when he confronts her with the stories Stanley has told him of her past. Mitch then forces Blanche to stand under the direct light. When he tells her that he doesn't mind her age, just her deceitfulness, Blanche responds by saying that she doesn't mean any harm. She believes that magic, rather than reality, represents life as it ought to be. Blanche's inability to tolerate light means that her grasp on reality is also nearing its end.

In Scene Six, Blanche tells Mitch that being in love with her husband, Allan Grey, was like having the world revealed in bright, vivid light. Since Allan's suicide, Blanche says, the bright light has been missing. Through all of Blanche's inconsequential sexual affairs with other men, she has experienced only dim light. Bright light, therefore, represents Blanche's youthful sexual innocence, while poor light represents her sexual maturity and disillusionment.

BATHING

Throughout *A Streetcar Named Desire,* Blanche bathes herself. Her sexual experiences have made her a hysterical woman, but these baths, as she says, calm her nerves. In light of her efforts to forget and shed her illicit past in the new community of New Orleans, these baths represent her efforts to cleanse herself of her odious history. Yet, just as she cannot erase the past, her bathing is never done. Stanley also turns to water to undo a misdeed when he showers after beating Stella. The shower serves to soothe his violent temper; afterward, he leaves the bathroom feeling remorseful and calls out longingly for his wife.

DRUNKENNESS

Both Stanley and Blanche drink excessively at various points during the play. Stanley's drinking is social: he drinks with his friends at the bar, during their poker games, and to celebrate the birth of his child. Blanche's drinking, on the other hand, is antisocial, and she tries to keep it a secret. She drinks on the sly in order to withdraw from harsh reality. A state of drunken stupor enables her to take a flight of imagination, such as concocting a getaway with Shep Huntleigh.

For both characters, drinking leads to destructive behavior: Stanley commits domestic violence, and Blanche deludes herself. Yet Stanley is able to rebound from his drunken escapades, whereas alcohol augments Blanche's gradual departure from sanity.

SYMBOLS

Symbols are objects, characters, figures, or colors used to represent abstract ideas or concepts.

SHADOWS AND CRIES

As Blanche and Stanley begin to quarrel in Scene Ten, various oddly shaped shadows begin to appear on the wall behind her. Discordant noises and jungle cries also occur as Blanche begins to descend into madness. All of these effects combine to dramatize Blanche's final breakdown and departure from reality in the face of Stanley's physical threat. When she loses her sanity in her final struggle against Stanley, Blanche retreats entirely into her own world. Whereas she originally colors her perception of reality according to her wishes, at this point in the play she ignores reality altogether.

THE VARSOUVIANA POLKA

The Varsouviana is the polka tune to which Blanche and her young husband, Allen Grey, were dancing when she last saw him alive. Earlier that day, she had walked in on him in bed with an older male friend. The three of them then went out dancing together, pretending that nothing had happened. In the middle of the Varsouviana, Blanche turned to Allen and told him that he "disgusted" her. He ran away and shot himself in the head.

The polka music plays at various points in *A Streetcar Named Desire,* when Blanche is feeling remorse for Allen's death. The first time we hear it is in Scene One, when Stanley meets Blanche and asks her about her husband. Its second appearance occurs when Blanche tells Mitch the story of Allen Grey. From this point on, the polka plays increasingly often, and it always drives Blanche to distraction. She tells Mitch that it ends only after she hears the sound of a gunshot in her head.

The polka and the moment it evokes represent Blanche's loss of innocence. The suicide of the young husband Blanche loved dearly was the event that triggered her mental decline. Since then, Blanche hears the Varsouviana whenever she panics and loses her grip on reality.

"IT'S ONLY A PAPER MOON"

In Scene Seven, Blanche sings this popular ballad while she bathes. The song's lyrics describe the way love turns the world into a "phony" fantasy. The speaker in the song says that if both lovers believe in their imagined reality, then it's no longer "make-believe." These lyrics sum up Blanche's approach to life. She believes that her fibbing is only her means of enjoying a better way of life and is therefore essentially harmless.

As Blanche sits in the tub singing "It's Only a Paper Moon," Stanley tells Stella the details of Blanche's sexually corrupt past. Williams ironically juxtaposes Blanche's fantastical understanding of herself with Stanley's description of Blanche's real nature. In reality, Blanche is a sham who feigns propriety and sexual modesty. Once Mitch learns the truth about Blanche, he can no longer believe in Blanche's tricks and lies.

MEAT

In Scene One, Stanley throws a package of meat at his adoring Stella for her to catch. The action sends Eunice and the Negro woman into peals of laughter. Presumably, they've picked up on the sexual innuendo behind Stanley's gesture. In hurling the meat at Stella, Stanley states the sexual proprietorship he holds over her. Stella's delight in catching Stanley's meat signifies her sexual infatuation with him.

SUMMARY & ANALYSIS

SCENE ONE

They told me to take a street-car named Desire, and
transfer to one called Cemeteries, and ride six blocks
and get off at—Elysian Fields!

(See QUOTATIONS, *p. 57*)

SUMMARY

The setting is the exterior of a corner building on a street called Elysian Fields, which runs between the river and the train tracks in a poor section of New Orleans that has "raffish [crude] charm." Faded white stairs lead up to the entrances of the shabby building's two flats. Steve and Eunice live upstairs, and Stanley and Stella live downstairs. The hum of voices in the street can be heard, as well as the bluesy notes of a cheap piano playing in a bar around the corner. (Williams notes that the music from this piano is to set the mood throughout the play.) It is an early May evening, and the sky at dusk is almost turquoise.

Eunice and a Negro woman are relaxing on the steps of the building when Stanley and his buddy Mitch show up. Stanley hollers for Stella, who comes out onto the first-floor landing and replies calmly to his tough, streetwise banter. He hurls a package of meat up to her and says that he and Mitch are going to meet Steve at the bowling alley. They depart, and Stella soon follows to watch them. Eunice and the Negro woman find something hilariously suggestive in the meat-hurling episode, and their cackles indicate sexual innuendo.

Soon after Stella leaves, her sister, Blanche, arrives, carrying a suitcase and looking with disbelief at a slip of paper in her hand and then at the building. Dressed in a fine white suit appropriate for an upper-crust social event, Blanche moves tentatively, looking and apparently feeling out of place in Stella's neighborhood. Eunice assures Blanche that the building is Stella's residence. When Blanche declines to go to the bowling alley, the Negro woman goes instead to tell Stella of her sister's arrival.

Eunice lets Blanche into the two-room flat, and Blanche investigates the interior of the Kowalskis' apartment. Making small talk,

Eunice mentions what she knows of Blanche from Stella—that Blanche is from Mississippi, that she is a teacher, and that her family estate is called Belle Reve. Tiring of Eunice's questions, Blanche asks to be left alone. Eunice, somewhat offended, leaves to fetch Stella.

Alone, Blanche sits looking nervous and uncomfortable as she surveys the messy, dingy surroundings. Spying a bottle of whiskey in the closet, she suddenly breaks out of her dejected stupor. She pours a healthy shot, downs it immediately, replaces the bottle, cleans her tumbler, and returns to her original pose.

Stella returns with excitement, and she and Blanche embrace. Blanche talks feverishly and seems nearly hysterical. After initially expressing her thrill at seeing her younger sister, Blanche lets slip a critical comment on the physical and social setting in which Stella lives. She tries to check her criticism, but the reunion begins on a tense note. Blanche redirects the conversation by asking if Stella has any liquor in the flat. She claims she could use the drink to calm her nerves, but insists—without being asked—that she isn't a drunk. After the drink is poured, Blanche asks how Stella has allowed herself to stoop to such poor living conditions. Stella makes a light effort to defend her present lifestyle, but she mostly lets Blanche do the talking.

Stella's quietness unnerves Blanche, who suggests that Stella isn't happy to see her. She then explains that she has come to New Orleans because her nerves have forced her to take a leave of absence from her job as a schoolteacher during the middle of the term. She asks Stella to tell her how she looks, fusses over Stella's plumpness and disheveled appearance, and is surprised to learn that Stella has no maid.

Blanche takes another drink, and then worries about the privacy and decency of her staying in the apartment with no door to separate her from Stella and Stanley in the next room. She worries that Stanley won't like her, and she makes several disparaging comments about Stanley's lower-class status, focusing on his Polish background. Stella warns Blanche that Stanley is very different from the men with whom Blanche is familiar back home. She is quite clearly deeply in love with him.

In an outburst that builds to a crescendo of hysteria, Blanche reveals that she has lost Belle Reve, the family's ancestral home. She recounts how she suffered through the agonizingly slow deaths of their parents and relatives, and points the finger at Stella for running off to New Orleans and leaving all familial woes behind. Stella finally cuts her off and leaves the room, crying. Stanley's return interrupts Blanche's apology.

Outside the apartment, Stanley discusses plans for poker the following day with Steve and Mitch. Mitch discourages their discussion of borrowing money and refuses to host poker at his mother's house. The men settle on playing poker at Stanley's, and Steve and Mitch leave.

Meanwhile, Blanche has been nervously moving through the apartment in anticipation of meeting Stanley. He enters the apartment, sizes Blanche up, and makes small talk with her, treating her casually while she nervously tries to engage with him. Stanley pulls the whiskey bottle out of the closet and notices that it is running low. He offers Blanche a drink, but she declines, saying that she rarely drinks. Stanley proceeds to change his sweaty T-shirt in front of Blanche, offending her modesty. All the while, Stella still hasn't emerged from the bathroom. When Stanley abruptly asks what happened to Blanche's marriage, Blanche replies haltingly that the "boy" died, then plops down and declares that she feels ill.

ANALYSIS

The play offers a romanticized vision of slum life that nevertheless reflects the atypical characteristics of New Orleans. The mix of characters and social elements around Elysian Fields demonstrates the way New Orleans has historically differed from other American cities in the South. It was originally a Catholic settlement (unlike most Southern cities, which were Protestant), and consequently typical Southern social distinctions were ignored. Hence, blacks mingle with whites, and members of different ethnic groups play poker and bowl together. Stanley, the son of Polish immigrants, represents the changing face of America. Williams's romanticizing is more evident in his portrayal of New Orleans as a city where upper-class people marry members of the lower class, fights get ugly but are forgotten the next day, and the perpetual bluesy notes of an old piano take the sting out of poverty.

The play immediately establishes Stanley and Blanche as polar opposites, with Stella as the link between them. Stage directions describe Stanley as a virulent character whose chief pleasure is women. His dismissal of Blanche's beauty is therefore significant, because it shows that she does not exude his same brand of carnal desire. On the other hand, Blanche's delicate manners and sense of propriety are offended by Stanley's brutish virility. Stanley's qualities—variously described as vitality, heartiness, brutality, primitiv-ism, lust for life, animality—lead him over the course of the play into an unrelenting, unthinking assault on the already crumbling facade of Blanche's world.

Blanche comes across as a frivolous, hysterical, insensitive, and self-obsessed individual as she derides her sister's lesser social status and doesn't express joy at seeing Stella so in love. Blanche, who arrives in New Orleans having lost Belle Reve and having been forced to leave her job, exudes vulnerability and emotional frailty. Stanley's cocky interactions with Blanche show him to be insensi-tive—he barely lets Blanche get a word in edgewise as he quickly assesses her beauty. Nevertheless, in this introduction, the audience is likely to sympathize with Stanley rather than Blanche, for Blanche behaves superficially and haughtily, while Stanley comes across as unpretentious, a social being with a zest for life.

Stanley's entrance with a package of meat underscores his primi-tive qualities. It is as if he were bringing it back to his cave fresh from the kill. His entrance also underscores the intense sexual bond between him and Stella, which is apparent to the other characters as well. Stanley yells "Catch!" as he tosses the package, and a moment later the Negro woman yells "Catch *what!*" Eunice and the Negro woman see something sexual, and scandalously hilarious, in Stan-ley's act of tossing the meat to a breathlessly delighted Stella.

The name of the Kowalskis' street underscores the extreme, oppos-ing archetypes that Stanley and Blanche represent. Elysian Fields is the name for the ancient Greek version of the afterlife. Stanley, the primi-tive, pagan reveler who is in touch with his vital core, is at home in the Elysian Fields, but the Kowalskis' home and neighborhood clearly are not Blanche's idea of heaven. Blanche represents a society that has become too detached from its animal element. She is distinctly overciv-ilized and has repressed her vitality and her sexuality. Blanche's health and her sanity are waning as a result.

SCENE TWO

SUMMARY

> *There are thousands of papers, stretching back over*
> *hundreds of years, affecting Belle Reve as, piece by*
> *piece, our improvident grandfathers and father and*
> *uncles and brothers exchanged the land for their epic*
> *fornications—to put it plainly!*
> (See QUOTATIONS, p. 58)

It is six o'clock in the evening on the day following Blanche's arrival. Blanche is offstage, taking a bath to soothe her nerves. When Stanley walks in the door, Stella tells him that in order to spare Blanche the company of Stanley's poker buddies in the apartment that night, she wants to take Blanche out, to New Orleans's French Quarter. Stella explains Blanche's ordeal of losing Belle Reve and asks that Stanley be kind to Blanche by flattering her appearance. She also instructs Stanley not to mention the baby.

Stanley is more interested in the bill of sale from Belle Reve. Stella's mention of the loss of Belle Reve seems to convince Stanley that Blanche's emotional frailty is an act contrived to hide theft. He thinks Blanche has swindled Stella out of her rightful share of the estate, which means that *he* has been swindled. In order to prove his own victimization, he refers to the Napoleonic code, a code of law recognized in New Orleans from the days of French rule that places women's property in the hands of their husbands.

Looking for a bill of sale, Stanley angrily pulls all of Blanche's belongings out of her trunk. To him, Blanche's glitzy evening dresses, feather boas, fur stoles, and costume jewelry look expensive, and he assumes she has spent the family fortune on them. He claims he'll have his friend come over to appraise the value of the trunk's contents. Enraged at Stanley's actions and ignorance, Stella storms out onto the porch.

Blanche finishes her bath and appears before Stanley in the kitchen wearing a red satin robe. She says that she feels clean and fresh, then closes the curtains to the bedroom in order to dress out of Stanley's sight. Stanley replies gruffly to Blanche's idle chatter. When she unashamedly asks him to come and fasten her buttons, he refuses. He begins to question sarcastically how Blanche came to acquire so many fancy dress items, and he rejects Blanche's flirtatious bids to make the conversation more kind-spirited. Sensing that the impending conversation might upset Stella, Blanche calls out to her sister requesting that she run to the drugstore to buy a soda.

Blanche takes from her trunk a box filled with papers and hands it to Stanley. Stanley snatches additional papers from her trunk and begins to read them. Blanche is horrified and grabs back this second set of papers, which are old letters and love poems she has saved from her husband. She redirects Stanley's attention to the papers she originally handed to him, and Stanley realizes that Blanche has acted honestly—the estate really was lost on its mortgage, not sold as he suspected.

Blanche describes the estate's decline. Her ancestors owned an enormous plantation, but the men so mishandled affairs with their "epic fornications" that only the house and a small parcel of land containing the family graveyard were left by the time Blanche and Stella were born. Blanche manages to disarm Stanley and convince him that no fraud has been perpetrated against anyone. Stanley lets slip that Stella is pregnant.

Stella returns from the drugstore, and some of the men arrive for their poker game. Exhilarated by the news of Stella's pregnancy and by her own handling of the situation with Stanley, Blanche follows Stella for their girls' night out. On their way offstage, Blanche comments that mixing their old, aristocratic blood with Stanley's immigrant blood may be the only way to insure the survival of their lineage in the world.

> Oh, I guess he's just not the type that goes for jasmine perfume, but maybe he's what we need to mix with our blood now that we've lost Belle Reve.
>
> (See QUOTATIONS, p. 59)

ANALYSIS

Scene Two starts to move our sympathies away from Stanley as the more malignant aspects of his character start to surface. Whereas Scene One stresses the sexual attraction that drew Stella and Stanley to one another despite class differences, Scene Two shows Stanley acting disrespectful to Stella and antagonistic to her sister. Meanwhile, our compassion for Blanche increases as Williams reveals just how destitute she is by showing that all of her belongings in the world amount to a trunk full of gaudy dresses and cheap jewelry.

In one sense, Stanley and Blanche are fighting for Stella—each would like to pull Stella beyond the reach of the other. But their opposition is also more elemental. They are incompatible forces—manners versus manhood—and peace between them is no more than a temporary cease-fire. Blanche represents the Old South's intellectual romanticism and dedication to appearances. Stanley represents the New South's ruthless pursuit of success and economic pragmatism. When Stanley confronts Blanche after her bath, she shows that she understands the nature of their clash when she tells him that Stella doesn't understand him as well as she does.

Calling upon the Napoleonic code enables Stanley to justify his feelings of entitlement toward Stella's inheritance. In doing so, he shows that he is ignorant of legal technicalities, because Belle Reve, located in Laurel, Mississippi, wouldn't fall under New Orleans jurisdiction. However, Stanley's repeated references to the Napoleonic code highlight the fact that his conflict with Blanche is also a gender showdown. Stanley's greed reveals his misogyny, or woman-hating tendencies. As a man, Stanley feels that what Stella has belongs to him. He also hates Blanche as a woman and as a person with a more prestigious family name, and therefore suspects that Blanche's business dealings have been dishonest.

Blanche takes the first of many baths in this scene. She claims that steaming hot baths are necessary to calm her nerves, a believable excuse given her constant hysteria. Yet Blanche's constant need to wash her body symbolizes her need for emotional, spiritual, and mental cleansing. Her bathing foreshadows the eventual revelation of her sordid past. She desires to rid herself of her social blemishes and start over after leaving Laurel.

Two mysteries from Scene One are solved in Scene Two. Blanche reveals the "boy" she spoke of at the end of Scene One to be her husband. She tells Stanley that she hurt her husband the way that Stanley would like to hurt her, warning him that his goal is impossible, since she is "not young and vulnerable anymore." Blanche knew her husband's weakness and unfeelingly used that weakness to destroy him. Yet she is naïve to think that Stanley won't be able to do the same thing to her. She would like to believe that her age and experience protect her against Stanley's callous assaults, but Stanley recognizes Blanche's essential weakness. Also, Stella's revelation to the audience that she is pregnant (when she asks Stanley not to mention her pregnancy to Blanche) explains Blanche's remark about Stella's weight gain, and Stella's refusal to discuss her weight gain with her sister.

SCENE THREE

SUMMARY

It is around 2:30 A.M. Steve, Pablo, Mitch, and Stanley are playing poker in the Kowalskis' kitchen, which is bathed in a sinister green light. Their talk is heavy with testosterone and the effects of whiskey, several glasses of which litter the table. Stanley dominates the table with his tough talk, while Mitch, who frets about whether or not he should go home to his sick mother, shows himself to be the most sensitive and sober man at the table. After exchanging a few harsh words with Stanley, Mitch rises from the table to go to the bathroom.

Stella and Blanche return. Blanche insists on powdering her face at the door of the house in anticipation of the male company. Stella makes polite introductions, but the men show no interest in Blanche's presence. When Stella asserts that it's time to stop playing for the night, Stanley refuses her request, tells her to go upstairs to Eunice's, and disrespectfully slaps her on the buttocks. Stella is shamed and joins Blanche, who is planning to take another bath, in the bedroom. Mitch emerges into the bedroom from the bathroom and is sheepish and awkward upon meeting Blanche, indicating that he is attracted to her. Once he has left the room, Blanche remarks that there is something "superior to the others" in Mitch. Stella agrees that Mitch is polite but claims that Stanley is the only one of them who will "get anywhere."

Stella and Blanche continue their sisterly chat in the bedroom while the poker game continues. Stanley, drunk, hollers at them to be quiet. While Stella is busy in the bathroom, Blanche turns on the radio, further angering Stanley. The other men enjoy the music, but Stanley springs up and shuts off the radio. He and Blanche stare each other down. Mitch skips the next hand to go to the bathroom again. Waiting for Stella to finish in the bathroom, he and Blanche talk. Blanche is a little drunk and unabashedly flirtatious. They discuss Mitch's sick mother, the sincerity of sick and sorrowful people, and the inscription on Mitch's cigarette case. Blanche fibs that she is actually younger than Stella, and that she has come to New Orleans because Stella is ailing and needs her assistance. She asks Mitch to put a Chinese lantern she has bought over the naked lightbulb. As they talk Stanley grows increasingly annoyed at Mitch's absence from the game.

Stella leaves the bathroom, and Blanche impulsively turns the radio back on and begins to dance, slyly engaging the clumsy Mitch and preventing his leaving to go to the bathroom. Stanley leaps up, rushes to the radio, and hurls it out the window. Stella yells at Stanley, and he advances violently toward her. He follows her as she runs offstage, and the stage directions call for sounds of him beating her. The other men pull him off. Stella cries out that she wants to get away, and Blanche scrambles to gather clothes and take Stella upstairs to Eunice's apartment. Mitch condemns Stanley's behavior to Blanche. Then the men attempt to revive the now limp and confused Stanley, but when they try to force him into the shower to sober him up, he fights them off. They grab their poker winnings and leave.

Stanley stumbles out of the bathroom, calling for Stella. He cries remorsefully and then telephones upstairs, but Eunice won't let him speak to Stella. After calling again to no avail, he hurls the phone to the floor. Then, half-dressed, he stumbles out to the street and calls for his wife again and again: "STELL- LAHHHHH!" Eunice warns him to stop, but his bellowing cry continues. Finally, a disheveled Stella slips out of the apartment and down to where Stanley is. They stare at each other and then rush together with "animal moans." He falls to his knees, tenderly caresses her face and belly, then lifts her up and carries her into their flat.

Blanche emerges from Eunice's flat, frantically looking for Stella. She stops short at the entrance to the downstairs flat. Mitch returns and tells her not to worry because Stella and Stanley are crazy about each other. He offers her a cigarette. She thanks him for his kindness and waxes poetic while he quietly listens.

SUMMARY & ANALYSIS

ANALYSIS

Scene Three underscores the primal nature of Stella and Stanley's union, and it cements Stanley's identity as a villain. After Stanley's drunken radio-hurling episode, Stella yells at him and calls him an "animal thing," inciting Stanley's attack. Later that night, Stanley bellows "STELL-LAHHHHH!" into the night like a wounded beast calling for the return of his mate. Their reunion is also described in terms of animal noises. Stanley's cruel abuse of his wife convinces the audience that genteel Blanche has her sister's best interests in mind more than Stanley does. Yet Stella sides with Stanley and his base instincts, infusing the play with an ominous sense of gloom.

Audience sympathy may establish itself in Blanche's favor, but nothing about Blanche suggests that she will emerge as a heroine.

The sense of mystery surrounding Blanche's peculiar arrival in New Orleans takes on a sinister taint, and Blanche's reluctance to be in bright light calls attention to this mysterious nature. Both metaphorically and literally, bright light threatens to undo Blanche's many deceptions. While conversing with Mitch, she asks him to place a Chinese lampshade on the bare lightbulb in the bedroom, claiming that the naked bulb is "rude" and "vulgar." Bright light, whether from a naked bulb or the midday sun, reveals Blanche's true age. She can claim to be a woman of twenty-five in semi-darkness, but the glare of sharp light reveals a woman who has seen more, suffered more, and aged more. In addition, probing questions and honest speech function as a metaphorical light that threatens to reveal Blanche's past and her true nature. Blanche is in no mental condition to withstand such scrutiny, so she has fashioned a tenuous make-believe world. Her effort to create a more flattering, untruthful portrait of herself for Mitch continues in upcoming scenes.

Mitch and Blanche clearly feel attracted to one another, perhaps because both have a broken quality as a result of their experiences with the death of loved ones. Blanche lost her husband and Mitch the girl who gave him the cigarette case with the poetic inscription. Both also nursed their parents through lingering deaths. However, whereas Mitch's experiences have engendered in him a strong sincerity, Blanche seeks refuge in make-believe and insincerity—insincerity that is painfully obvious in her remarks about the sincerity of dying people. The difference in their reactions to similar experiences and in their approaches to life suggests that they are not an ideally matched pair. Blanche thinks on a spiritual level, while Mitch behaves practically and temperately. When they dance, we see that they are ill suited to one another even on a physical level—Mitch dances clumsily, awkwardly mimicking Blanche's grand movements.

Prior to Scene Three, the piano music that sounds throughout the play functions chiefly to create atmosphere, suggesting the play's setting in a somewhat seedy section of New Orleans. Over the course of the poker game and the Kowalskis' fight, however, the piano's sound changes, registering the turbulent emotional shifts of the action onstage. For example, discordant sounds play as the violent drama heightens.

SCENE FOUR

SUMMARY

The morning after the poker game, Stella lies serenely in the bedroom, her face aglow. Her satiated appearance contrasts strongly with that of Blanche, who, haggard and terrified, tiptoes into the messy apartment. Blanche is greatly relieved to find Stella safe and sound. She demands to know how Stella could go back and spend the night with Stanley after what he did to her. Stella feels Blanche is making a big issue out of nothing, claiming that she likes Stanley the way he is. She explains that Stanley's violence is the type of bad habit you have to learn to put up with from other people, and she adds that Stanley has always been violent—on their honeymoon, he smashed all of the lightbulbs with her shoe. Blanche is horrified, but Stella refuses to listen and cheerily proceeds to start cleaning the apartment.

Blanche's horror intensifies, and she begins to rant that she and Stella need to find a way out of their situation. She recounts how she recently ran into an old suitor named Shep Huntleigh who struck it rich in oil—perhaps he would be able to provide the money they need to escape. Blanche begins to compose a telegram to Shep, and when Stella laughs at her for being ridiculous, Blanche reveals that she is in fact completely broke. Stella offers her five dollars of the ten that Stanley gave her as an apology that morning. She says she has no desire to leave and that Blanche merely saw Stanley at his worst. Blanche retorts that she saw Stanley at his best, because "what such a man has to offer is animal force," but she argues that it's impossible for herself to live with such a man.

Blanche simply cannot understand how a woman raised at Belle Reve could choose to live her life with such an ungentlemanly, brutish man. Stella replies that her physical relationship with Stanley "make[s] everything else seem—unimportant." Blanche argues that sheer desire is no basis for a marriage. Stella hints that Blanche is familiar with the pleasure of gratifying her desire. Blanche agrees that she has done so, but she adds that she wouldn't settle down with a man whose primary attraction is sexual.

A train approaches, and while it roars past Stanley enters the flat unheard. Not knowing that Stanley is listening, Blanche holds nothing back and describes Stanley as a common, apelike, primitive brute. Stella listens coldly. Under cover of another passing train,

Stanley slips out of the apartment, and enters it again noisily. Stella runs to Stanley and embraces him fiercely. Stanley grins at Blanche.

ANALYSIS

Although Stella technically condemns Stanley's propensity for violence, it is clear to Blanche and to the audience that Stanley's violent behavior heightens Stella's desire for him. When Stella tells Blanche that Stanley broke all the lightbulbs with her shoe on their honeymoon, Blanche is horrified, but Stella assures her that she found the episode "thrilling." Even the stage directions at the beginning of Scene Four, which liken Stella's glowing face after a night spent with Stanley to that of an Eastern idol, suggest there is a mystical aspect to Stanley and Stella's violent attraction. Stella calmly lies in bed at the scene's opening as if she has just taken part in something holy.

When telling Stella that sheer desire is no basis for a marriage, Blanche points out that there is a streetcar in New Orleans named "Desire" that "bangs through the [French] Quarter, up one old narrow street and down another." She invokes the streetcar as a metaphor for what she believes Stella feels. Stella asks whether Blanche has ever ridden on the streetcar, and Blanche's answer, "It brought me here," foreshadows later events in the play. As Stella, Stanley, and Mitch soon learn, Blanche's wanton acts of desire are indeed what led to her expulsion from life in Laurel, Mississippi. In fact, her family's attitude toward desire began to push her toward her present predicament even before she was born. The family's socially regulated need to shroud desire and cover up "epic fornications" led to the breakup of the Belle Reve estate and to the impoverishment of the present generation.

Scene Four reveals Blanche to be entirely calculating when it comes to her relations with men. As she rambles on about money, Shep Huntleigh, and other things, she rejects Stella's imperative that she "Talk sense!" by insisting, "I've got to keep thinking." This comment suggests that Blanche survives by scheming up ways to get money from men. Blanche's threat to "laugh in [Stella's] face" if Stella tries to claim that her attraction to Stanley is "just one of those electric things" shows that Blanche does not truly believe in love. Throughout the play, Blanche claims to possess romantic notions of timeless relations, but her comments to Stella in this scene reveal her as a cold cynic.

Scene Four also contains one of Blanche's most famous speeches, in which she describes how humankind has evolved too far past the beast that Stanley represents for Stella to reduce herself to his level.

This passage best articulates Williams's examination of the widely held belief among plantation owners and their descendants that the end of the South's agrarian culture led to a decline of American civilization. He depicts Blanche as an antiquated relic of a dead society, while Stanley epitomizes the new type of American, who lacks refinement, education, and spirituality. Yet, although Williams gives voice to Blanche's nostalgia and exposes her fears, he does not necessarily share her belief that the new Americans are lesser beings on the evolutionary scale. He even illustrates the irrationality of Blanche's opinions by having her hysterically cry to Stella, *"Don't— don't hang back with the brutes!"*

SCENE FIVE

SUMMARY

Stella and Blanche are in the bedroom on an August afternoon. Blanche breaks out in laughter at the untruthfulness of the letter she has just finished writing to Shep Huntleigh, prompting Stella to ask her about the letter's contents. Blanche gleefully reads the letter aloud. In it, she suggests that she visit Shep in Dallas, and she claims that she and Stella have been amusing themselves with society parties and visits to luxurious country homes. Stella finds no humor in her sister's stories.

Their conversation is interrupted by the sound of Steve and Eunice fighting upstairs. Eunice accuses Steve of infidelity and cries out as he begins to beat her. After a huge noise, Eunice runs out of her flat, yelling that she is going to the police. Stanley, returning home from bowling, asks Stella why Eunice is so distraught. Stella says that Eunice has had a fight with Steve, and she asks whether Eunice is with the police. Stanley replies that he has just seen her at the bar around the corner, having a drink. Stella responds lightheartedly that alcohol is a "more practical" cure than the police for Eunice's woes. Steve comes downstairs nursing a bruise on his forehead, inquires after Eunice's whereabouts, and grumpily hurries off to the bar.

In the Kowalski apartment, Stanley and Blanche have a tense conversation. Blanche makes superficially charming comments to Stanley that subtly insult his lower-class disposition. Stanley is unusually rude to Blanche. He insinuates that he has acquired knowledge of Blanche's past and asks her if she knows a certain man named Shaw. Blanche falters immediately at the mention of Shaw's name and answers evasively, replying that there are many Shaws in the world. Stanley goes on to say that the Shaw he met often travels to Blanche's hometown of Laurel, Mississippi, and that Shaw claims Blanche was often the client of a disreputable hotel. Blanche fiercely denies Stanley's accusation and insists that Shaw must have confused her with someone else. Stanley says he will check with Shaw the next time he sees him. Eunice and Steve stroll back to their apartment, affectionately wrapped in each other's arms. Stanley then heads off to the bar, telling Stella to meet him there.

Stanley's remarks leave Blanche horribly shaken, but Stella doesn't seem to notice. Blanche demands to know what people in town have been saying about her, but Stella has no idea what Blanche is talking about. Blanche confesses that she has behaved badly during the past two years, the period when she was losing Belle Reve. She criticizes herself for not being self-sufficient and describes herself as "soft," claiming that she has to rely on Chinese lanterns and light colors to make herself "shimmer and glow." She then admits that she no longer has the youth or beauty to glow in the soft light.

Offering Blanche a soda, Stella responds that she doesn't like to hear such depressing talk. Blanche says that she wants a shot of alcohol to put in the Coke. She tries to get it herself, but Stella insists on waiting on her, claiming that she likes to do so because it reminds her of their childhood. Blanche becomes hysterical and promises to leave soon, before Stanley throws her out. Stella calms her for a moment, but when she accidentally spills a little soda on Blanche's skirt, Blanche lets out a shriek.

Blanche tries to laugh off the fact that she is shaking, claiming that she feels nervous about her date that evening with Mitch. She explains that she hasn't been honest with him about her age and that she feels she lacks the forces of attraction her youthful beauty once provided her. She has not gone to bed with him because she wants Mitch's respect, but she's worried he will lose interest in her. She is convinced that she must maintain her act if Mitch is to love her. She wants him very badly and says she needs him as a stabilizing force—and as her ticket away from Elysian Fields. As Stanley comes around the corner, yelling for Stella, Steve, and Eunice, Stella assures Blanche that everything will work out. She gives Blanche a kiss and then runs off to join Stanley at the bar. Eunice and Steve run after her.

Sipping her drink, Blanche sits alone in the apartment and waits for Mitch. A young man comes to the door to collect money for the newspaper. Blanche flirts with him, offers him a drink, and launches a seduction. The young man is uncomfortable and nervous. Blanche declares that he looks like an Arabian prince, then kisses him on the lips and sends him on his way, saying, "I've got to be good—and keep my hands off children." A few moments later, Mitch appears with a bunch of roses. Blanche accepts the flowers with much fanfare, while Mitch glows.

ANALYSIS

Although Stella's reassurance and comforting of Blanche about her relationship with Mitch is a rare moment of unchecked affection between the two sisters, by not revealing her past Blanche prevents Stella's full comprehension of the desperate nature of Blanche's situation. Even without Stanley around to prevent free and open communication, Blanche cannot bring herself to explain her belief that Mitch is her last chance of salvation from ruin. Because Stella does not know the full weight of the baggage Blanche is carrying, she cannot provide the advice and support Blanche needs, and she simply expresses hope that Mitch will bring Blanche the same contentment that Stanley brings her.

When she throws herself at the young newspaper boy, Blanche reveals her hypocrisy—she is lustful underneath her genteel, morally upright facade. Blanche condemns Stanley and Stella's purely sexual relationship, but we see that her urges are every bit as strong as Stella's, yet much less appropriate. Compared with Blanche's behavior, Stella's love life looks healthy and wholesome. Eunice and Steve's quick reconciliation after their fight also underscores the notion that Stella and Stanley's violent love is the norm in these parts. Like the sexual attachment between Stella and Stanley, Eunice and Steve's sexual attachment appears far healthier than Blanche's, and Blanche's expectations for love begin to seem unrealistic. As a dramatic device, the scene with the newspaper boy prepares us to learn the truth about the circumstances surrounding Blanche's departure from Mississippi. She is one of the "epic fornicators" of her clan, the last in a line of aristocrats who secretly indulged in forbidden acts because they could not find a stable outlet for their desires. When a bumbling Mitch arrives at the apartment for his date with Blanche, he quickly becomes an antidote to Blanche's strong carnal desires.

As the identity Blanche has constructed for herself begins to disintegrate, she begins to lose ground in her battle against Stanley. Stanley's questioning of Blanche about her acquaintanceship with Shaw is the play's first direct mention of Blanche's blemished past.

Blanche does a poor job of pretending not to know Shaw. Her claim that she needs to avoid revealing her past to Mitch further supports our suspicions about her truthfulness. Up to this point, Blanche's jitteriness and her need to hide herself from the outside world have suggested that she also had a past to hide. Now, the emerging facts of Blanche's past begin to confirm the hypocrisy of her social snobbery.

SCENE SIX

SUMMARY

Around 2 A.M., Blanche and Mitch return to the Kowalski flat after their date. The large plastic statuette that Mitch carries suggests their date took place at an amusement park. Blanche appears completely wiped out. Mitch is more awake but clearly melancholy. He apologizes for not giving her much entertainment during their evening, but Blanche says it was her fault that she simply couldn't manage to enjoy herself. She reveals that she will be leaving the flat soon. When Mitch asks if he may kiss her goodnight, she tells him he doesn't have to ask permission. He points out that she responded negatively when he had tried for a bit more "familiarity" when they parked his car by the lake one night. Blanche explains that though Mitch's attraction flatters her, a single girl becomes "lost" if she doesn't keep her urges under control. She teases Mitch, suggesting that he is used to women who are easy on their first date. Mitch tells Blanche that he likes her because she is different from anyone he has ever met, an independent spirit. Blanche laughs and invites him in for a nightcap.

Blanche lights a candle and prepares the drinks, saying they must celebrate and forget their worries on their last night together. She suggests that they pretend to be on a date at an artists' café in Paris. She asks Mitch if he speaks French. After he tells her he doesn't, she teases him in the language he can't understand, asking, "Do you want to sleep together this evening? You don't understand? What a shame!" Blanche grows rapidly more amorous. Mitch won't take his coat off because he's embarrassed about his perspiration, so she takes it off for him. She tries to put Mitch at ease by admiring his imposing physique. When he asks her what she weighs, she tells him to guess. He picks her up, and the game leads to a brief and somewhat clumsy embrace. Blanche stops him from putting any more moves on her, claiming she has "old-fashioned ideals." She sarcastically rolls her eyes as she offers this remark, but Mitch cannot see her face.

After an uncomfortable silence, Mitch asks where Stanley and Stella are, and he suggests that they all go out on a double date some night. Blanche laughs at the idea, and asks how Mitch and Stanley became friends. Mitch replies that they were military buddies. Blanche asks what Stanley says about her, expressing her conviction that Stanley hates her. Mitch thinks that Stanley simply doesn't understand her. Blanche argues that Stanley wants to ruin her.

Mitch interrupts Blanche's increasingly hysterical tirade against Stanley to ask her how old she is. Caught off guard, she responds by asking why he wants to know. He says that when he told his ailing mother about Blanche, who would like to see Mitch settled before she dies, he could not tell her how old Blanche was. Blanche says that she understands how lonely Mitch will be when his mother is gone. She fixes another drink for herself and gives a revealing account of what happened with the tender young man she married. She was only sixteen when they met, and she loved him terribly. Somehow, though, her love didn't seem to be enough to save him from his unhappiness—something was tormenting him. Then one day she came home to find her young husband in bed with an older man who had been his longtime friend. In the hours after the incident, they all pretended nothing happened. The three of them went out to a casino. On the dance floor, while dancing a polka, the Varsouviana, she drunkenly confronted her young husband and told him he "disgusted" her. The boy rushed out of the casino, and everyone heard a shot. He had killed himself with a bullet to the head.

Mitch comes to her and holds her, comforting her. He tells her, "You need somebody. And I need somebody, too." They kiss, even as she sobs. Blanche says, "Sometimes—there's God—so quickly!"

ANALYSIS

Blanche's encounter with Mitch exposes her sexual double standard. In secret, she bluntly attempts to seduce the young man collecting for the newspaper, an interaction that happens outside the boundaries of acceptable or even reasonable behavior. Because the incident is so far removed from Blanche's professed moral standards, she feels free to behave as she likes without fear. In contrast, since the Kowalskis and their neighbors know of Blanche's outings with Mitch, she believes that they must take place within the bounds of what she sees as social propriety.

Blanche's revelation of the story of her first love occurs in a heavily symbolic manner. Blanche describes her all-consuming first love in terms of lightness and darkness, using the concept of light to explain her interior state as she does earlier in the play. She says that when she fell in love, the once-shadowy world seemed suddenly illuminated with a "blinding light." She extends the metaphor when she describes the aftermath of her thoughtless, cruel remark to her husband, saying, "[T]he searchlight . . . was turned off again and never for one moment since has there been any light that's stronger than this—kitchen—candle." We see in earlier scenes that a lack of light has enabled Blanche to live a lie, but now we see also that, without light, Blanche has lived without a clear view of herself and reality.

The music of the Varsouviana that plays in the background during Blanche's story is also symbolic. Blanche mentions that the Varsouviana was playing as she told her husband that he disgusted her, and the music represents Blanche's memory of her husband's suicide. When the polka surfaces from this point on, it signals that Blanche is remembering her greatest regret and escaping from the present reality into her fantasy world. Blanche's husband's suicide was the critical moment in her life, the moment she lost her innocence.

Mitch's lack of formal manners and education make him an imperfect match for Blanche, but he and Blanche are able to relate on a ground of common suffering and loneliness. Though she is clearly the object of Mitch's affection, he is the one with the upper hand in the relationship. Blanche needs Mitch as a stabilizing force in her life, and if her relationship with him fails, she faces a world that offers few prospects for a financially challenged, unmarried woman who is approaching middle age. Unfortunately, though Blanche lets down her flippant guard and confesses her role in her husband's suicide to Mitch at the scene's close, her failure to be upfront about her age, her entire past, and her intentions signals doom for her relationship with him. She tacitly admits that she needs Mitch when she accepts his embrace, but her fears of acknowledging reality overpower her and prevent her from telling the full truth.

SCENE SEVEN

SUMMARY
Stella is decorating her apartment on an afternoon in mid-September. Stanley comes in, and Stella explains to him that it is Blanche's birthday. Blanche is in the bathroom, taking yet another hot bath to calm her nerves. Stanley makes fun of Blanche's habit of taking baths, but Stella admonishes him. She points out that she and

Blanche grew up differently than he did, but he says he won't stand for that excuse any longer. He tells Stella to sit down and listen—he has dirt on Blanche. Blanche's unconcerned voice issues from the bathroom as she sings the sugary popular ballad "It's Only a Paper Moon."

Stanley has learned the shady details of Blanche's past from Shaw, a supply man he works with who regularly travels to Blanche and Stella's hometown of Laurel, Mississippi. Gleefully, Stanley recounts how Blanche earned a notorious reputation after taking up residence at the seedy Flamingo Hotel. The hotel asked her to leave, presumably for immoral behavior unacceptable even by the standards of that establishment. She came to be regarded as crazy person by the townspeople, and her home was declared off-limits to soldiers at a nearby base. She was not given a leave of absence by her school—she was kicked out after a father reported his discovery that Blanche was having a relationship with a seventeen-year-old boy. Stanley surmises that Blanche, having lost her reputation, her place of residence, and her job, had no choice but to wash up in New Orleans. He is certain that she has no intention of returning to Laurel.

Stanley's stories don't fully convince Stella. She admits that Blanche has her problems, but explains them as the result of Blanche's tragic young marriage to a homosexual man. Stanley asks Stella how many candles she's putting in Blanche's cake, and Stella says she'll "stop at twenty-five." She says that Mitch has been invited, but Stanley abashedly says not to expect Mitch to show up. Stanley says it was his duty to reveal the truth about Blanche to his army friend and bowling teammate. He has told Mitch the bad news about Blanche, and there's no way Mitch will marry her now. Stella is horrified because both she and Blanche had been convinced Mitch and Blanche would marry.

Stanley tells Stella that he has bought Blanche a birthday present: a one-way bus ticket back to Laurel. He yells at Blanche to get out of the bathroom. When at last Blanche emerges, she is in high spirits, until she sees Stanley's face as he passes by. He goes into the bathroom and slams the door. Blanche senses from Stella's dazed responses to her chatter that something is wrong. She asks Stella what has happened, but Stella feebly lies and says that nothing has happened.

ANALYSIS

It is difficult to assess whether Stanley or Blanche herself is more to blame for Blanche's ruin, which is sealed by the end of Scene Seven. To some extent, Blanche brought her fate upon herself by leading a promiscuous and almost deranged life, in spite of the genteel morality to which she pays lip service. But Blanche's desire and her hypocrisy do not absolve Stanley of his vindictive pursuit of Blanche's vulnerabilities. Stanley is shortsighted and unsympathetic, as we can see in his inability to understand why the story of Allan Grey, Blanche's lost husband, moves Stella so deeply. To Stanley, the fact that Blanche's husband committed suicide renders her a weak rather than sympathetic person.

Stanley's behavior toward Blanche seems even crueler once he reveals that Blanche is not just flighty and sensitive but also mentally unsound. In addition to proving Blanche's hypocrisy, the stories Stanley tells Stella about Blanche introduce the first outright reference to Blanche's mental state. Describing what he's heard from Shaw, Stanley declares that in Laurel Blanche is seen as a crazy woman.

Blanche's interminable baths function as a metaphor for her need to cleanse herself of her sordid past and reputation. She emerges from them refreshed and temporarily renewed. Stanley's repeated objections to Blanche's baths, ostensibly because he would like to urinate, function on a metaphorical level to show his rejection of Blanche's make-believe purification, which allows her to pretend modesty and put on airs without acknowledging reality.

The lyrics of "It's Only a Paper Moon," the popular 1940s ballad Blanche sings while bathing, summarize Blanche's situation with regard to Mitch. She sings, "It's a Barnum and Bailey world / Just as phony as it can be / But it wouldn't be make-believe / If you believed in me." Blanche's hope in a future with Mitch rests in his believing her act—or in his believing in her strongly enough to make the act reality. Williams juxtaposes Blanche's merry rendition of this song with Stanley's malicious revelations about her character, creating a situation of tense dramatic irony as Blanche sings about a future that will never come to fruition. The song describes the fanciful way one perceives the world while in love, but it also foreshadows the fact that Mitch falls out of love with Blanche after his illusions about her have been destroyed.

SCENE EIGHT

SUMMARY

> *People from Poland are Poles, not Polacks. But what I*
> *am is a one hundred percent American, born and raised*
> *in the greatest country on earth and proud as hell of it,*
> *so don't ever call me a Polack.*
>
> *(See* QUOTATIONS, *p. 60)*

Forty-five minutes later, Blanche's gloomy birthday dinner is wind-ing down. The place set for Mitch remains empty. Blanche tries to break the gloomy silence by asking Stanley to tell a funny story. He declines, so Blanche tells a lame joke involving a priest and a swear-ing parrot. Stanley makes a point of not laughing. Instead, he reaches across the table for a chop and eats it with his fingers. Stella scolds him for having greasy fingers and orders him to help clean up. He smashes his plate and declares that he is sick and tired of being called derogatory names such as "greasy." He orders both sisters never to forget that he is the king of his house. He smashes his cup and saucer, yells that he has cleared his place, and storms out onto the porch. Stella begins to cry. Blanche again asks Stella what happened while she was taking a bath, but Stella says that nothing happened.

Blanche declares that she will call Mitch to find out why he didn't attend her dinner. Stella implores her not to, but Blanche goes into the bedroom to make the call. Stella joins Stanley on the porch. Blanche leaves a message—Mitch is not home—and stays by the phone, looking frightened. Stanley holds Stella, ignoring her reproaches, and promises her that things will be all right again after Blanche leaves and the baby comes. Stella goes back inside and lights the candles on the cake. Blanche and Stanley join her.

Blanche announces that she should never have called Mitch and that she doesn't need to take insults from a man like him. Stanley begins to complain about the lingering heat from Blanche's steam bath, and she snaps that she has already apologized three times. She says that a healthy Polack like Stanley wouldn't understand her need to calm her nerves. Stanley angrily retorts that Polish people are called Poles, not Polacks, and that he is "one hundred percent American."

The phone rings, and Blanche tries to answer it, expecting Mitch. Stanley intercepts her and speaks to the caller, one of his bowling buddies. While Stanley speaks on the phone, Stella touches Blanche on the shoulder. Blanche, confused and angered by Stella's unexplained pitying behavior, tells Stella to back off. Stanley erupts, yelling for Blanche to be quiet. She tries her best to control herself as Stanley returns to the table. With a thin veneer of kindness, Stanley offers Blanche a birthday present. She is surprised and delighted—until she opens it and sees that it is a one-way ticket back to Laurel on a Greyhound bus, leaving Tuesday.

The Varsouviana music begins to play as Blanche tries first to smile, then to laugh. When her efforts fail, she runs to the bedroom and then to the bathroom, clutching her throat and making gagging noises as if Stanley's cruelty has literally taken her breath away. Stanley, pleased with himself and his actions, prepares to go bowling. But Stella demands to know why Stanley has treated Blanche so callously. She admits that much about Blanche is insufferable, but argues that Blanche's naïve trust and kindness have been abused over the years, and that the current Blanche is the product of suffering. He explains that Stella thought he was common when they first met, but he took her off her pedestal, and things were wonderful until Blanche arrived and made fun of him. As he speaks, a sudden change comes over Stella, and she slowly shuffles from the bedroom to the kitchen. After a minute, Stanley notices that something is wrong and cuts his diatribe short. Stella quietly asks to be taken to the hospital. Stanley is with her in an instant, speaking softly as he leads her out the door.

Analysis

In Scene Eight, Stanley, Blanche, and Stella become increasingly short-tempered. Stanley shows that he has taken all that he can handle of Blanche and will allow Stella to sway him with her protestations no longer. He is intent on removing Blanche from his house, and he sees no need for delicacy or kindness in doing so. However, Blanche too seems to have reached the limit of her capacity for niceness. She loses her temper briefly when she snaps to Stanley that she has already apologized three times for her bath. Her outburst constitutes the first time Blanche openly express anger in the play.

Stella too becomes increasingly assertive as she begs Stanley to explain his contempt for Blanche and to attempt to understand Blanche's nature. She insists that Stanley not leave to go bowling and demands an explanation from him for his cruelty to Blanche. These actions constitute the greatest assertion of independence Stella makes toward Stanley throughout the entire play. As Stella grows angrier, her grammar becomes more formal, and she uses words such as "needn't." Stanley's grammar, on the other hand, grows sloppier, and he begins to speak in sentence fragments. The language Stella and Stanley use indicates their respective retreats away from each other into their social roles. But just when Stella seems to be thinking independently from Stanley and reasserting her connection to Blanche in her outrage at Stanley's cruelty, she goes into labor. The baby reasserts Stella's connection to Stanley and makes Stella dependent on him for help. He is once again in control as he takes her to the hospital.

Stella does not recognize her own similarities with Blanche. Her comments to Stanley as she begs him to understand Blanche's situation show that she views Blanche with pity. Yet, when making her case to Stanley, Stella argues that Blanche was trusting in her youth until "people like you abused her." Even though Stella recognizes that Blanche was worn down by "people like" Stanley, she does not reject him or realize that she could wind up in Blanche's place. Stanley, however, reminds Stella of her similarity to Blanche when he points out that he had to pull Stella down from the columns of Belle Reve.

Stanley's discussion of his and Stella's relationship as a response to Stella's demand to know why he is so cruel to Blanche seems strange. He begins by asking Stella if she remembers when she found him "common," and states that after he pulled Stella down from the columns of Belle Reve, he and Stella were happy to be "common" together until Blanche showed up. The implication of Stanley's speech is that he desires to take ownership of people and things, like Blanche and Stella, that make him feel inferior. What Stanley doesn't understand is how precarious and insecure the once majestic world of Belle Reve was by the time Stella and Blanche were born. His actions toward Blanche are all the more cruel because he misunderstands how weak Blanche is to begin with. Stanley's desire for ownership manifests itself as the furious sexual desire he displays for Stella in the play. The heated passion of Stanley's marriage foreshadows his enraged violence toward Blanche, which also expresses his need for ownership, but in a different form.

Scene Nine

Summary

Later the same evening, Blanche sits tensely in the bedroom. On a nearby table are a bottle of liquor and a glass. The Varsouviana, the polka music that was playing when Blanche's husband killed himself, can be heard. Williams's stage directions state that the music we hear is in Blanche's head, and that she drinks to escape it.

Mitch, unshaven and wearing work clothes, comes to the door. The doorbell startles Blanche. She asks who it is, and when he gruffly replies, the polka music stops. She frantically scurries about, applying powder to her face and stashing the liquor in a closet before letting Mitch in with a cheerful reprimand for having missed her birthday celebration. She expects a kiss, but Mitch walks right past her into the apartment. Blanche is frightened but continues in her light and airy mode, scolding him for his disheveled appearance and forgiving him in the same breath.

Mitch, a bit drunk, stares and then asks Blanche to turn off the fan, which she does. He plops down on the bed and lights a cigarette. She offers him a drink, fibbing that she isn't sure what the Kowalskis have on hand, but Mitch says he doesn't want Stanley's liquor. Blanche retorts that she's bought her own liquor, then changes the subject to Mitch's mother's health. Mitch is suspicious of Blanche's interest in his mother, so she backs off, saying she just wants to know the source of Mitch's sour mood. As Blanche retreats into herself, the polka music again begins in her head, and she speaks of it agitatedly, identifying it as the same tune that was playing when her husband, Allan, killed himself. She breaks off, then explains that the usual sound of a gunshot, which makes the music stop, has come. Mitch has no idea what Blanche is talking about and has little patience for her anxiety.

As Blanche rambles on about the birthday evening Mitch missed, she pretends to discover the whiskey bottle in the closet. She takes her charade so far as to ask what Southern Comfort is. Mitch says the bottle must be Stan's, and he rudely rests his foot on Blanche's bed. Blanche asks Mitch to take his foot off the bed and goes on about the liquor, pretending to taste it for the first time. Mitch again declines a drink and says that Stanley claims Blanche has guzzled his liquor all summer on the sly.

At last Blanche asks point-blank what is on Mitch's mind. Mitch continues to beat around the bush, asking why the room is always so dark. He comments that he has never seen Blanche in full light or in the afternoon. She has always made excuses on Sunday afternoons and has only gone out with him after six to dimly lit places. Blanche says she doesn't get Mitch's meaning, and he says that he's never had a good look at her. Mitch tears the paper lantern off the lightbulb. She begs him not to turn the light on, but he says that he wants to be "realistic." Blanche cries that she doesn't like realism and "want[s] magic." She explains that her policy is to say what "ought" to be true. Mitch switches the light on, and Blanche lets out a cry and covers her face. He turns the light off.

Mitch says he doesn't really care about Blanche's age, but he cannot stand the way Blanche lied to him all summer, pretending to be old-fashioned and morally upright. Blanche tries to deny Mitch's charge, but Mitch says that he has heard stories about her from three different sources: Stanley, Shaw, and a merchant from Laurel named Kiefaber with whom Mitch spoke on the phone. Each man presented the same facts about Blanche's shady past. Blanche argues that all three men are liars, and that Kiefaber concocted stories about her as revenge for her spurning his affection.

Finally, Blanche breaks down and admits the truth through convulsive sobs and shots of liquor. She says that she panicked after Allan's death and looked to strangers for human companionship to fill her loneliness. She did not know what she was doing, she claims. She eventually ended up in trouble with a seventeen-year-old student from Laurel High School and was forced to leave her position. She thought she had nowhere to go, until she met Mitch. He gave her hope because he said he needed her as she needed him. But, says Blanche, she was wrong to hope, because her past inevitably caught up with her. After a long pause, Mitch can say only that Blanche lied to him, "inside and out." Blanche argues that she didn't lie "inside . . . in [her] heart."

A blind Mexican woman comes around the corner selling bunches of tacky tin flowers to use at funerals. In Spanish, she says, "Flowers. Flowers for the dead." Hearing the vendor's voice, Blanche opens the door, and she is terrified when the woman offers her funeral flowers. She slams the door and runs back into the apartment as the vendor continues down the street. The Varsouviana polka tune resumes.

Blanche begins to think out loud while Mitch sits silently. Every so often, the Mexican woman's call can be heard. In her tortured soliloquy, Blanche discusses regrets, and then legacies. She speaks about pillowcases stained with blood, and seems to be recalling a conversation she had with her mother about not having enough money to pay a servant. Blanche then begins to speak about death, saying that it once seemed so far from her. She says that "the opposite [of death] is desire." And she begins to reminisce about camp of soldiers that used to be near Belle Reve. On Saturday nights the drunken soldiers would stumble onto Blanche's lawn and call for her while her deaf mother slept. Occasionally, Blanche went outside to meet them.

The polka music fades. Mitch approaches Blanche and tries to embrace her. He says that he wants what he waited for all summer. Blanche says he must marry her first, but Mitch replies that Blanche isn't fit to live in the same house as his mother. Blanche orders him to leave, rapidly collapsing into hysterics. When he does not move, she threatens to scream "Fire!" He still does not leave, so she screams out the window. Mitch hurries out, and Blanche falls to her knees, devastated. Piano music can be heard in the distance.

ANALYSIS

Mitch's act of turning on Blanche's light explicitly symbolizes his extermination of the fake persona she has concocted. Mitch recognizes that Blanche's deceptions have relied on darkness to obscure reality, thereby giving Blanche the freedom to describe things as she feels they "ought to be." For example, in Scene Six, Blanche revises reality by lighting a candle, claiming that she and Mitch will be bohemian and imagine they are in Paris.

Mitch behaves with resignation rather than anger when he confronts Blanche, showing that he holds genuine feelings for her. He initially bides his time, getting up the nerve to say what he has come to say. Sadness over lost love tempers his anger and frustration. When Mitch turns on Blanche's light, he violates Blanche's false dignity, but he does not violate Blanche sexually when she refuses him. However, his advances demonstrate that the only way he knows how to express his frustration over the relationship ending is through sexuality.

Whereas Mitch faces his breakup with Blanche with resignation, Blanche becomes desperate and unhinged. She sees marriage as her only means of escaping her demons, so Mitch's rejection amounts to a sentence of living in her internal world. Once Mitch crushes the make-believe identity Blanche has constructed for herself, Blanche begins to descend into madness. With no audience for her lies, which Blanche admits are necessary when she tells Mitch that she hates reality and prefers "magic," Blanche begins performing for herself. Yet Blanche's escapist tendencies no longer manifest her need to live in a world full of pleasant bourgeois ease. Instead of fancy and desire, her new alternate reality reflects regret and death. She is alone, afraid of both the dark and the light; her own mind provides her with a last bastion of escape. Her fantasies control her, not the other way around, but still she shrinks from the horror of reality.

Scene Nine fails to tell us conclusively whether Blanche is responsible for her fate or whether she is a victim of circumstances beyond her control. Mitch claims that it is Blanche's lying, not her age, that bothers him. Indeed, it is likely Mitch figures out that Blanche is past her prime in Scene Six, when she evades his questions about her age. Given Mitch's statement, it seems that Blanche's sexual duplicity and romantic delusions have been the source of her fall. Yet Blanche is also the victim of social circumstances. She was born into a society that required the suppression of desire, and her sense of entitlement, to wealth and social status, elicit the anger of new Americans in an increasingly diverse social landscape. Additionally, Blanche is Stanley's victim. His investigations of her past and his disclosure of his findings contribute directly to Blanche's fate.

Scene Ten

Summary

It is a few hours after Mitch's departure. Blanche's open trunk sits with clothes hanging out of it in the middle of the bedroom. Blanche sits before the mirror, places a tiara on her head, and speaks out loud, flirting with imaginary suitors. She speaks of boozing and carousing after a late-night party. A closer glance at herself in a hand mirror quickly upsets her, and she angrily smashes the mirror.

Stanley enters the apartment, slamming the door behind him and giving a low whistle when he sees Blanche decked out in an old white satin evening gown and jeweled party shoes. Like Blanche, Stanley is drunk, and he carries several unopened beer bottles. Blanche asks about Stella, and Stanley tells her the baby won't be born until the following day. They will be the only two in the apartment that night.

With mock politeness, Stanley asks why Blanche is all dressed up. She tells him that Shep Huntleigh, a former admirer, has sent her a telegram inviting her to join him on his yacht in the Caribbean. She explains that she has nothing suitable to wear on a cruise. Stanley seems happy for Blanche. As he takes off his shirt, Blanche requests that he close the curtains before finishing undressing, but Stanley says that he's done for the moment. He opens a bottle of beer on the corner of the table, then pours the foam on his head. He suggests that he and Blanche each have a beer to celebrate their good news—

his new baby and her millionaire. Blanche declines Stanley's offer, but his good spirits persist.

In anticipation of good news from the hospital, Stanley goes to the bedroom to find his special silk pajamas. Blanche continues to talk about Shep Huntleigh, feverishly working herself up as she describes what a gentleman he is and how he merely wants the companionship of an intelligent, spirited, tender, cultured woman. Blanche claims that though she is poor financially, she is rich in spirit and beautiful in mind. She asserts that she has been foolishly lavishing what she has to offer on those who do not deserve it—"casting [her] pearls before swine."

At the word "swine," Stanley's amicable mood evaporates. Blanche continues, recounting how Mitch arrived earlier that night to accuse her of the slanderous lies that Stanley told him. Blanche claims that after she sent Mitch away, he came back in vain, with roses and apologies. She says that she cannot forgive "deliberate cruelty," and that the two of them are too different in attitude and upbringing for their relationship to work.

Stanley disrupts Blanche's story to ask if Mitch came by before or after her telegram from Shep Huntleigh. Blanche is caught off guard and forgets what she has said about Shep's telegram, and Stanley jumps on her mistake. He launches an attack, tearing down her make-believe world point by point. It turns out that Stanley saw Mitch after his encounter with Blanche, so Stanley knows that Mitch is still disgusted with her. All Blanche can say in reply is "Oh!" Stanley finishes his accusation of Blanche with a disdainful laugh and walks through the bedroom into the bathroom.

Frightening, sinister shadows and reflections begin to appear on the walls, mimicking Blanche's nervous movements. Wild, jungle-sounding cries can be heard. Blanche goes to the phone and desperately tries to make a call to Shep Huntleigh for help. She does not know his number or his address, so the operator hangs up on her. Blanche leaves the phone off the hook and walks into the kitchen.

The back wall of the Kowalskis' apartment suddenly becomes transparent, revealing the sidewalk, where a drunkard and a prostitute scuffle until a police whistle sounds and they disappear. Soon thereafter, the Negro woman comes around the corner rifling through the prostitute's purse.

Even more panicked, Blanche returns to the phone and whispers to the operator to connect her to Western Union. She tries to send a telegraph saying that she needs help desperately and is "[c]aught in a trap," but she breaks off when Stanley emerges from the bathroom in his special pajamas. He stares at her, grinning, while the phone begins to beep. He crosses the room and replaces the phone on the hook. Still grinning, he steps between Blanche and the door. The sound of the piano becomes louder and then turns into the sound of a passing train, disturbing Blanche. When the noise ends, she asks Stanley to let her pass by, and he takes one step to the side. She asks him to move further away, but he stays put and laughs at Blanche for thinking that he will try to prevent her from leaving.

The jungle voices swell as Stanley slowly advances toward Blanche, ignoring her cries that he stay away. She grabs a bottle and smashes its end on the table, threatening to smash the remaining fragment on Stanley's face. He jumps at her, grabs her arm when she swings at him, and forces her to drop the bottle. "We've had this date from the beginning," he says, and she sinks to her knees. He picks her up and carries her to the bed. The pulsing music indicates that Stanley rapes Blanche.

ANALYSIS

Williams mimics classical tragedy by not showing Blanche's rape, the play's climax and most violent act. The omission of the rape heightens our sense of its offensiveness and also reflects the notions of acceptable stage behavior held by Americans in 1947, when *A Streetcar Named Desire* was first produced. Our sense of the rape's inevitability is another reason why it seems unnecessary that the act take place onstage. Stanley's final statement to Blanche that they have "had this date from the beginning" suggests that his rape of her has been fated all along. Instead of an act of force, he casts what happens as the endgame of their elemental struggle against each other.

The way Stanley terrorizes Blanche by shattering her self-delusions parallels and foreshadows his physical defeat of her. Increasingly, Blanche's most visceral experiences are the delusions and repressed memories that torment her, so that her physical rape seems an almost inevitable consequence of her psychological pain. The rape also symbolizes the final destruction of the Old South's genteel fantasy world, symbolized by Blanche, by the cruel but vibrant present, symbolized by Stanley. In the New South, animal instinct and common sense win out over lofty ideals and romantic notions.

Williams indicates the impending rape through Stanley's macho, imposing, animalistic body language. Like a snake, Stanley flicks his tongue at Blanche through his teeth. He corners her in the bedroom, refusing to move out of her way, then "springs" at her, calling her a "tiger" as he captures her. Blanche's silent resignation as Stanley carries her to the bed indicates the utter defeat of her will.

Our opinion of Stanley has changed greatly by this second-to-last scene. At the start of the play, Stanley is more likable and down-to-earth than Blanche. He lacks her pretension, and he represents the new America, where reward is based on merit and good work, not on birth into fortunate circumstances. But Stanley's rape of Blanche just before his child is born, when he is at his most triumphant and she at her most psychologically vulnerable, is the ultimate act of cruelty. If rape is realism, then surely Blanche's world of dreams and fantasies is a better alternative. To confirm the terrible nature of reality, the back of Blanche's make-believe world falls away, and the world of the street, with its prostitution, drinking, and thievery, impinges upon her surroundings. Each of these three characters—the prostitute, the drunkard, and the thief—reflects to Blanche an aspect of her personality.

Scene Eleven

Summary

> *Whoever you are—I have always depended on the*
> *kindness of strangers.*   *(See* Quotations, *p. 61)*

A few weeks later, Stella cries while packing Blanche's belongings. Blanche is taking a bath. Stanley and his buddies are playing poker in the kitchen, which the stage directions describe as having the same ghastly atmosphere as on the poker night when Stanley beat Stella. Eunice comes downstairs and enters the apartment. Stanley boasts about his own ability to survive and win out against others thanks to his spectacular confidence, and Mitch stammers incoherently in angry disbelief.

Eunice calls the men callous and goes over to Stella to see how the packing is going. Stella asks how her baby is, and Eunice says the baby is asleep. Eunice asks about Blanche, and Stella says they have arranged for Blanche to spend some time resting in the country, but Blanche thinks she is going to travel with Shep Huntleigh. Blanche emerges from the bathroom briefly, asking Stella to tell any callers that she'll phone them back shortly. She requests that Stella find her yellow silk suit and its accessories, then returns to the bathroom. Stella tells Eunice that she isn't certain she did the right thing, but that there is no way she could believe Blanche's story about the rape and continue to live with Stanley. Eunice comforts Stella, saying she had no choice but to doubt Blanche's story and continue life as usual with Stanley.

Blanche opens the bathroom door hesitantly, checking to make sure that the men playing poker won't be able to see her as she comes out. She emerges with a slightly unhinged vivacity to the strains of the Varsouviana polka. Stella and Eunice behave in a gentle, accommodating manner. Blanche asks if Shep Huntleigh has called, and Stella answers, "[N]ot yet."

At the poker table, the sound of Blanche's voice sends Mitch into a daydream, until Stanley snaps him out of it. The sound of Stanley's voice from the kitchen stuns Blanche. She remains still for a few moments, mouthing Stanley's name, then with a rising hysteria demands to know what is going on. The women quiet and soothe her, and the men restrain Stanley from interfering. Blanche is appeased for the moment, but frantically anxious to leave. The other women convince her to wait. They offer her grapes, and she worries about whether they have been washed. Blanche starts to leave, but the women detain her again. They manage to hold her in the bedroom by playing on her fear of walking in front of the men at the poker table, saying she should wait until the game is over. Blanche lapses into a reverie about her upcoming vacation, imagining that she will die at sea from eating a dirty grape with a handsome young ship's doctor at her side.

The doorbell rings, and Blanche waits tensely, hoping that the caller is Shep Huntleigh, her savior. In reality, a doctor and nurse are at the door. Eunice returns and announces that someone is calling for Blanche, saying she thinks it might be Shep. Blanche becomes tense, and the Varsouviana begins again. When Eunice mentions that a lady accompanies Blanche's caller, Blanche grows more nervous. She frets again about walking in front of the poker players, but Stella accompanies her. The poker players stand uncomfortably as Blanche passes, except for Mitch, who stares at the table. When Blanche steps out onto the porch and sees the doctor, not Shep Huntleigh, she retreats in fright to where Stella is standing, then slips back into the apartment.

Inside, Stanley steps up to block Blanche's way to the bedroom. Blanche rushes around him, claiming she has forgotten something. The weird reflections and shadows reappear on the walls, and the Varsouviana music and jungle cries grow louder. The doctor sends the nurse in after Blanche. In stage whispers, Stanley advises the doctor to go in, and the doctor tells the nurse to grab Blanche. As the nurse speaks to Blanche, her voice echoes eerily. Blanche panics and asks to be left alone. Stanley says the only thing Blanche could have possibly forgotten is her paper lantern, which he tears from the lightbulb and hands to her. Blanche shrieks and tries to escape. The nurse holds Blanche, who struggles in her grasp.

Stella bolts out onto the porch, and Eunice goes to comfort her. Stella begs Eunice to stop the group from hurting Blanche, but Eunice won't let Stella go. She tells Stella that she has made the right decision. The men move toward the bedroom, and Stanley blocks Mitch from entering. When Mitch goes to strike Stanley, Stanley pushes him back, and Mitch collapses in tears at the table. The doctor takes off his hat and approaches Blanche gently. At Blanche's soft request, the doctor tells the nurse to release Blanche, and that a straitjacket won't be necessary. The doctor leads Blanche out of the bedroom, she holding onto his arm. "Whoever you are," Blanche says, "I have always depended on the kindness of strangers."

The doctor leads Blanche through the kitchen as the poker players look on. Stella, crouched on the porch in agony, calls out her sister's name as she passes by. Blanche allows herself to be led onward and does not turn to look at Stella. The doctor, the nurse, and Blanche turn the corner and disappear. Eunice brings the baby to Stella and thrusts it into her arms, then goes to the kitchen to join the men. Stanley goes out onto the porch and over to Stella, who sobs while holding her child. Stanley comforts Stella with loving words and begins to caress her. In the kitchen, Steve deals a new hand.

ANALYSIS

Blanche's behavior toward the poker players and during her bath reflects the way being raped by Stanley has scarred her. At the start of the play, she performs for Stanley's friends and demands their charm and devotion. By its end, she wants to hide from their gaze and hopes they won't notice her. Blanche spends much of Scene Eleven in the bath, but the bathing in this scene is different than before—an attempt to wash away Stanley's recent violation rather than her past sexual acts. She also bathes to prepare for her imagined meeting with Shep Huntleigh rather than for any real encounter with a man. Blanche's bath in this scene shows her cleansing herself for an impending ritual and hiding from real danger rather than simply calming her nerves. It is clear that Stanley has destroyed Blanche's already tenuous connection to reality. She no longer hopes that reality will prove itself adaptable to her dreams.

Blanche's illusions and deceptions about her past lose out to the disturbing reality of the Kowalskis' marriage, but by the end of the scene the marriage proves to be a sort of illusion, based on deception. The two sisters' roles reverse. Stella admits that she may have entered a world of make-believe when she acknowledges that she cannot believe Blanche's story about the rape and continue to live with Stanley. Blanche, by retreating into hysteria and madness, and by refusing to acknowledge her sister as she leaves the apartment with the doctor, may be sparing Stella the horror of having to face the truth about her husband. Blanche's descent into madness shields Stella from the truth. If Blanche were to remain lucid, Stella might have to give Blanche's claims credibility.

In many of his plays, Williams depicts unmarried, fallen, Southern women such as Blanche who are victims to society's rules. The desperate nature of Blanche's situation is apparent in her mental attempts to convince herself that the chivalric gentleman still exists in the form of Shep Huntleigh. Her quiet determination to depend "on the kindness of strangers" is funny, because in the past Blanche has slept with quite a few strangers, but it also indicates the resignation and defeat women in her position must accept when it comes to counting on their families. Most of the strangers we see in the play—the newspaper boy, the Mexican flower woman—show that they have very little other than sadness to offer Blanche. Social convention in the Old South diminishes unmarried women completely, leaving them vulnerable to domination or destruction by men. By showing the triumph of brutality and ruthlessness over gentility and delicacy, this scene captures and portrays the disposable nature of Blanche's kind.

When she insists that Stella's life with Stanley must go on, Eunice argues that male companionship is a woman's means of survival in the face of social convention. Eunice believes that Stella must work fiercely to maintain her relationship with Stanley. Given what the audience sees Stella and Eunice suffer at the hands of their husbands, it is unlikely that these women believe *nothing* of Blanche's story. However, acknowledging its truth would require them to acknowledge their husbands' brutality, and it would interfere with their survival. Life "going on" depends on having the social protection of marriage and a family, regardless of the cost.

Stella's "luxurious" tears at the end of the play are shed not only for her sister, but also for the complexity and tension between illusion and reality, between Blanche's story and Stella's own understanding of her life. Stella cannot believe Blanche's story, but she cannot completely deny it either. Ultimately, Stella cries for herself, for Blanche, and for the fact that a part of her is glad to see Blanche go. She accepts the overdone comfort Stanley offers, which is peppered with endearments like "now, love," and which conforms to the script Stella needs for life to go on. An offstage announcement that another poker game ("seven-card stud") is about to commence ends the play with a symbol of the deception and bluffing that has taken place in the Kowalski house. The play's last line also serves as a subtle reminder that the nature of the game in the Kowalski household can always change.

IMPORTANT QUOTATIONS EXPLAINED

1. They told me to take a street-car named Desire, and transfer
    to one called Cemeteries, and ride six blocks and get off at—
    Elysian Fields!

Blanche speaks these words to Eunice and the Negro woman upon
arriving at the Kowalski apartment at the beginning of Scene One.
She has just arrived in New Orleans and is describing her means of
transportation to her sister's apartment. The place names that Williams uses in *A Streetcar Named Desire* hold obvious metaphorical
value. Elysian Fields, the Kowalskis' street, is named for the land of
the dead in Greek mythology. The journey that Blanche describes
making from the train station to the Kowalski apartment is an alle-
gorical version of her life up to this point in time. Her illicit pursuit
of her sexual "desires" led to her social death and expulsion from
her hometown of Laurel, Mississippi. Landing in a seedy district
that is likened to a pagan heaven, Blanche begins a sort of afterlife,
in which she learns and lives the consequences of her life's actions.

2.   There are thousands of papers, stretching back over
      hundreds of years, affecting Belle Reve as, piece by piece,
      our improvident grandfathers and father and uncles and
      brothers exchanged the land for their epic fornications—to
      put it plainly! . . . The four-letter word deprived us of our
      plantation, till finally all that was left—and Stella can verify
      that!—was the house itself and about twenty acres of
      ground, including a graveyard, to which now all but Stella
      and I have retreated.

Blanche gives this speech to Stanley in Scene Two after he accuses
her of having swindled Stella out of her inheritance. While showing
Stanley paperwork proving that she lost Belle Reve due to foreclo-
sure on its mortgage, Blanche attributes her family's decline in fortune to the debauchery of its male members over the generations.
Like Blanche, the DuBois ancestors put airs of gentility and refinement while secretly pursuing libidinous pleasure.

   Blanche's explanation situates her as the last in a long line of
ancestors who cannot express their sexual desire in a healthy fash-
ion. Unfortunately, she is forced to deal with the bankruptcy that is
the result of her ancestors' profligate ways. By running away to New
Orleans and marrying Stanley, Stella removed herself from the elite
social stratum to which her family belonged, thereby abandoning all
its pretensions, codes of behavior, sexual mores, and problems.
Blanche resents Stella's departure and subsequent happiness. In
Blanche's eyes, Stella irresponsibly left Blanche alone to deal with
their family in its time of distress.

3.   Oh, I guess he's just not the type that goes for jasmine
      perfume, but maybe he's what we need to mix with our
      blood now that we've lost Belle Reve.

In Scene Two, Blanche makes this comment about Stanley to Stella. Blanche's statement that Stanley is "not the type that goes for jasmine perfume" is her way of saying that he lacks the refinement to appreciate fine taste as Blanche can. She suggests that, under normal circumstances, he would be an inadequate mate for a member of the DuBois clan because of his inability to appreciate the subtler things in life, whether material or spiritual, jasmine perfume or poetry.

Yet the second half of Blanche's comment acknowledges that the DuBois clan can no longer afford luxuries or delude themselves with ideas of social grandeur. Since financially Blanche and Stella no longer belong to the Southern elite, Blanche recognizes that Stella's child unavoidably will lack the monetary and social privilege that she and Stella enjoyed. The genteel South in which Blanche grew up is a thing of the past, and immigrants like Stanley, whom Blanche sees as crude, are rising in social status. Like Stanley, Stella's child may lack an appreciation for perfume and other fineries, but Stanley will likely imbue him with the survival skills that Blanche lacks. The fact that Blanche's lack of survival skills ultimately causes her downfall underscores the new importance such skills hold.

QUOTATIONS

4.   I am not a Polack. People from Poland are Poles, not
      Polacks. But what I am is a one hundred percent American,
      born and raised in the greatest country on earth and proud
      as hell of it, so don't ever call me a Polack.

Blanche makes derogatory and ignorant remarks about Stanley's
Polish ethnicity throughout the play, implying that it makes him stu-
pid and coarse. In Scene Eight, Stanley finally snaps and speaks these
words, correcting Blanche's many misapprehensions and forcefully
exposing her as an uninformed bigot. His declaration of being a
proud American carries great thematic weight, for Stanley does
indeed represent the new American society, which is composed of
upwardly mobile immigrants. Blanche is a relic in the new America.
The Southern landed aristocracy from which she assumes her sense
of superiority no longer has a viable presence in the American econ-
omy, so Blanche is disenfranchised monetarily and socially.

QUOTATIONS

5.   Whoever you are—I have always depended on the kindness
       of strangers.

These words, which Blanche speaks to the doctor in Scene Eleven,
form Blanche's final statement in the play. She perceives the doctor
as the gentleman rescuer for whom she has been waiting since arriving in New Orleans. Blanche's final comment is ironic for two rea-
sons. First, the doctor is not the chivalric Shep Huntleigh type of
gentleman Blanche thinks he is. Second, Blanche's dependence "on
the kindness of strangers" rather than on herself is the reason why
she has not fared well in life. In truth, strangers have been kind only
in exchange for sex. Otherwise, strangers like Stanley, Mitch, and
the people of Laurel have denied Blanche the sympathy she deserves.
Blanche's final remark indicates her total detachment from reality
and her decision to see life only as she wishes to perceive it.

KEY FACTS

FULL TITLE
A Streetcar Named Desire

AUTHOR
Tennessee Williams

TYPE OF WORK
Play

GENRE
Tragedy

LANGUAGE
English

TIME AND PLACE WRITTEN
Late 1940s, New Orleans

DATE OF FIRST PUBLICATION
1947

PUBLISHER
New Directions

TONE
Ironic and sympathetic realism

SETTING (TIME)
1940s

SETTING (PLACE)
New Orleans, Louisiana

PROTAGONIST
Blanche DuBois

MAJOR CONFLICT
Blanche DuBois, an aging Southern debutante, arrives at her sister's home in New Orleans hoping to start a new life after losing her ancestral mansion, her job, and her reputation in her hometown of Laurel, Mississippi. Blanche's brother-in-law, a macho working-class guy named Stanley Kowalski, is so filled with class resentment that he seeks to destroy Blanche's character

in New Orleans as well. His cruelty, combined with Blanche's fragile, insecure personality, leaves her mentally detached from reality by the play's end.

RISING ACTION

Blanche immediately rouses the suspicion of Stanley, who (wrongly) suspects Blanche of swindling Stella out of her inheritance. Blanche grows to despise Stanley when she sees him drunkenly beat her pregnant sister. Stanley permanently despises Blanche after he overhears her trying to convince Stella to leave Stanley because he is common. Already suspicious of Blanche's act of superiority, Stanley researches Blanche's past. He discovers that in Laurel Blanche was known for her sexual promiscuity and for having an affair with a teenage student. He reports his findings to Blanche's suitor, Mitch, dissuading Mitch from marrying Blanche.

CLIMAX

After Stanley treats Blanche cruelly during her birthday dinner, giving her a bus ticket back to Laurel as a present, Stella goes into labor. She and Stanley depart for the hospital, leaving Blanche alone in the house. Mitch arrives, drunk, and breaks off his relationship with Blanche. Blanche, alone in the apartment once more, drowns herself in alcohol and dreams of an impossible rescue. Stanley returns to the apartment from the hospital and rapes Blanche.

FALLING ACTION

Weeks after the rape, Stella secretly prepares for Blanche's departure to an insane asylum. She tells her neighbor Eunice that she simply couldn't believe Blanche's accusation that Stanley raped her. Unaware of reality, Blanche boasts that she is leaving to join a millionaire suitor. When the doctor arrives, Blanche leaves after a minor struggle, and only Stella and Mitch, who sits in the kitchen with Stanley's poker players, seem to express real remorse for her.

THEMES

Fantasy's inability to overcome reality; the relationship between sex and death; dependence on men

MOTIFS

Light; bathing; drunkenness

KEY FACTS

SYMBOLS

Shadows and cries; the Varsouviana polka; "It's Only a Paper Moon"; meat

FORESHADOWING

In Scene Ten, Williams takes a brief detour away from events in the Kowalski household to show a street scene involving a prostitute, her male admirer, and a Negro woman. The man follows the prostitute solicitously, there is a struggle offstage, and then the Negro woman runs away with the prostitute's handbag. This scene foreshadows Stanley's rape of Blanche, which occurs offstage at the scene's end. Stanley's raiding of Blanche's trunk in Scene Two also foreshadows the rape.

KEY FACTS

Study Questions & Essay Topics

Study Questions

1. *What does Williams's depiction of Blanche and Stanley's lives say about desire?*

As its title indicates, *A Streetcar Named Desire* explores the destinations to which desire leads. In following their respective desires, Blanche and Stanley end up in very different places. Blanche is the victim of a culture that has unhealthily repressed its connection to primal and natural urges. Blanche's culture also forbids love to cross boundaries of class, race, and "normal" gender relationships. This means that, for Blanche, all but a narrow realm of sex is illicit, demonized, and taboo. The suppressed desire of Blanche and her forebears erupted from time to time in "epic fornications." Blanche's ancestors paid for their lust with their wealth, and Blanche pays with her sanity.

The interclass bond between Stanley and Stella, on the other hand, is animal and spiritual rather than intellectual or practical. Blanche cannot understand why her sister would enter into such a rough-and-tumble union, because Blanche has never reconciled her genteel identity with her own profound desire. The divide between her aristocratic sense of self and the "animal" urges that have at times controlled her is too great. Instead, Blanche invents a reality that conveniently ignores her own sexuality, her own vitality. She knows that a streetcar named *Desire* brought her to her present predicament, but intellectually she separates that desire from herself.

Williams advocates a moderate approach to the indulgence of desires. Desire is a fact of life and a driving force in the lives of Williams's characters. Though Stanley, a rapist and wife beater, is no one's prototype for the perfect man, Blanche's denial of her desire, which leads her to hit on young boys, is equally dangerous.

2. *The plot of* A STREETCAR NAMED DESIRE *is driven by the dueling personalities of Blanche and Stanley. What are the sources of their animosity toward one another?*

The most obvious difference between Blanche and Stanley is one of social background. Whereas Blanche comes from an old Southern family and was raised to see herself as socially elite, Stanley comes from an immigrant family and is a proud member of the working class. They meet one another in the socially turbulent postwar period in New Orleans, one of America's most diverse cities. Each represents values that are antagonistic to the other's chance at success in the modern world.

Within the play, Stella's loyalty serves as a symbol of that societal success. Blanche attempts to convince Stella to leave Stanley because she was born for better society and values, while Stanley keeps Stella in his grasp through his unpretentious, powerful sexual attraction. The basic differences in Blanche's and Stanley's social stations and relationship to Stella expand into larger issues that make compromise impossible.

Blanche and Stanley are polar opposites in several respects. Blanche clearly represents the world of fantasy. As she admits to Mitch, she wants to misrepresent things, and she wants things misrepresented to her. She lives for how things ought to be, not for how they are. She prefers magic and shadows to facing facts in bright light. Stanley, on the other hand, is a no-nonsense, cut-to-the-chase kind of guy. He looks for joy in life, and where he finds it, he celebrates it. But, as he says, he expects people to lay their cards on the table. He has no patience for idle chit-chat, social compliments, fools, and frauds.

Blanche repeatedly refers to Stanley and his world as brutish, primitive, apelike, rough, and uncivilized. Stanley finds this sort of superiority offensive and says so, but there *is* something primal and brutish about Stanley. By contrast, Blanche represents civilization on the decline. She speaks vaguely of art, music, and poetry as proof of progress, but reveals little true knowledge. Blanche does not give Stanley credit for any higher feelings, but Stanley dislikes Blanche because of her unwillingness to reconcile herself to her own "lower" feelings.

3. A STREETCAR NAMED DESIRE *can be described as an elegy, or poetic expression of mourning, for an Old South that died in the first part of the twentieth century. Expand on this description.*

The story of the DuBois and Kowalski families depicts the evolving society of the South over the first half of the twentieth century. The DuBois clan, embodied in the play by Blanche, represents the genteel society of the Southern plantation owners that presided through the nineteenth century. Stanley Kowalski, the son of Polish immigrants, descends from new Southerners. He works in a factory and is therefore engaged in the industrialization of the South, which contributed to the demise of the agrarian society in which Blanche and Stella were raised. The play demonstrates that Stanley is well adapted for survival in the New South, represented by the diverse city of New Orleans, while Blanche is unable to survive in the new society.

Blanche and Stella are remnants of Southern aristocracy's decadence. The family's material resources have been swallowed up, and all that remain are its manners and pretensions. Blanche deludes herself and imagines she lives in a world in which manners and pretensions are still relevant. Stella, however, has turned her back on her ancestors and married someone who would have been considered below her station by her own people. Stanley is new blood, for a new South in transition. But Williams portrays Stanley as possessing a fare share of brutality, suggesting that the changing world in which Stanley fits so perfectly is not necessarily a kind one. The struggle for survival has replaced gentility, and Blanche is an inevitable loser in this struggle.

The events of the play's conclusion represent the death of the Old South. Unable to cope or to find a way to support herself since the loss of Belle Reve, Blanche goes mad and departs from reality. Stella sustains herself through her marriage and sexual union with Stanley. Stella and Stanley's newborn child, a mixture of immigrant American and Southern American heritage, represents the South's future.

SUGGESTED ESSAY TOPICS

1. Describe the use of light in the play. What does its presence or absence indicate?

2. How does Williams use sound as a dramatic device?

3. How does Blanche's fascination with teenage boys relate to her decline and fall?

4. Compare and contrast Mitch to the other men in the play.

5. Compare and contrast Blanche and Stella.

REVIEW & RESOURCES

QUIZ

1. What subject did Blanche teach at Laurel High School?

   A. English
   B. Music
   C. Social Studies
   D. Math

2. How does Mitch verify the stories Stanley tells him about Blanche?

   A. He speaks with Stella
   B. He speaks with the principal of Blanche's school
   C. He speaks with a supply man named Shaw and a merchant named Kiefaber
   D. He doesn't verify them

3. Where does Stanley see Eunice after her fight with Steve?

   A. At the police station
   B. With Stella in the Kowalski apartment
   C. Sitting on the steps with the Negro woman
   D. At the local bar

4. Where does Blanche meet Mitch?

   A. At the local bar
   B. At the Kowalskis' apartment
   C. At the bowling alley
   D. In a Paris hotel

5. Which of the following songs does Blanche sing while taking a bath?

   A. "It's Only a Paper Moon"
   B. "Twinkle, Twinkle, Little Star"
   C. "The Michigan Rag"
   D. "Desire"

6. What poet does Williams quote in the epigraph to *A Streetcar Named Desire*?

    A.   Wallace Stevens
    B.   Hart Crane
    C.   Walt Whitman
    D.   Emily Dickinson

7. Which of the following bonds is not shared by Mitch and Stanley?

    A.   They served in the army together
    B.   They play poker together
    C.   They work at the same automotive parts company
    D.   They are each married to a DuBois sister

8. What type of music was playing when Blanche's young husband committed suicide?

    A.   An Irish jig
    B.   A waltz
    C.   A polka
    D.   A fugue

9. Where is Shep Huntleigh from?

    A.   Spain
    B.   New Orleans
    C.   Dallas
    D.   Kansas City

10. Stella left Belle Reve after the death of which family member?

    A.   Her mother
    B.   Her aunt
    C.   Her father
    D.   Her brother

11. Which of the following events occurs first?

    A.   Eunice gets in a fight with Steve
    B.   Blanche kisses the Young Collector
    C.   Stella goes into labor
    D.   Blanche meets Mitch

12. Which of the following accurately describes Elysian Fields?

    A. Ethnically diverse, working class, quiet
    B. Mostly white, working class, noisy
    C. Ethnically diverse, working class, noisy
    D. Mostly Hispanic, middle class, sparsely populated

13. What does Blanche say caused her family to lose Belle Reve?

    A. Her ancestors' "epic fornications"
    B. Her ancestors' dependence on slave labor
    C. Her father's death
    D. Her mother's "spendthrift ways"

14. What does Blanche pretend to find when Mitch comes by while Stella is in labor?

    A. Liquor
    B. Her bath salts
    C. A candle
    D. A gun

15. Who lives upstairs from Stanley and Stella?

    A. The Negro woman
    B. No one
    C. Mitch and his mother
    D. Steve and Eunice

16. What does Stella profess she likes to do for her sister?

    A. Dress her
    B. Serve her
    C. Write letters
    D. Set up dates

17. What does Blanche give the Young Collector?

    A. Money
    B. A kiss
    C. A stern warning
    D. Retribution

REVIEW & RESOURCES

18. Which of the following does not function as a symbol in *A Streetcar Named Desire*?

    A. Beer
    B. Lamplight
    C. The Varsouviana polka tune
    D. Meat

19. Why is Blanche grateful to the doctor in the final scene?

    A. He found her missing keys
    B. He agrees with her claim that Stanley is a scoundrel
    C. He delivered Stella's baby
    D. He is a kind stranger

20. What doesn't Blanche know?

    A. Shep Huntleigh's phone number and address
    B. Where the liquor is in the Kowalski apartment
    C. Where the Flamingo Hotel is
    D. How to tie her shoes

21. Where is Stella when Blanche first arrives at Elysian Fields?

    A. At the local bar
    B. At the bowling alley
    C. At the drugstore
    D. At the doctor's

22. Why did Blanche leave her job as a schoolteacher in Laurel?

    A. She found it boring
    B. She had an affair with a young male student
    C. Her children needed her at home
    D. Stella invited her to spend several months in New Orleans

23. What material is Mitch's jacket made from?

    A. Alpaca
    B. Satin
    C. Silk
    D. Goose down

24. What sound does Blanche always hear before the Varsouviana music in her head stops?

    A. The cry of a baby
    B. The roar of a tiger
    C. The bang of a gunshot
    D. The trickle of running bathwater

25. What does Stanley buy Blanche for her birthday?

    A. A tiara
    B. A bowling jacket
    C. A bus ticket
    D. A bottle of Southern Comfort

ANSWER KEY:
1: A; 2: C; 3: D; 4: B; 5: A; 6: B; 7: D; 8: C; 9: C; 10: C; 11: D; 12: C; 13: A; 14: A; 15: D; 16: B; 17: B; 18: A; 19: D; 20: A; 21: B; 22: B; 23: A; 24: C; 25: C

SUGGESTIONS FOR FURTHER READING

BLOOM, HAROLD, ed. *A Streetcar Named Desire.* New York: Chelsea House Publishers,1988.

———. *Tennessee Williams.* New York: Chelsea House Publishers, 1987.

GRIFFIN, ALICE. *Understanding Tennessee Williams.* Columbia: Universityof South Carolina Press, 1995.

LEVERICH, LYLE. *Tom: The Unknown Tennessee Williams.* New York: Crown Publishers,Inc., 1995.

LONDRE, FELICIA HARDISON. *Tennessee Williams.* New York: Frederick Ungar PublishingCo., 1979.

O'CONNOR, JACQUELINE. *Dramatizing Dementia: Madness in the Plays of Tennessee Williams.* Bowling Green, Ohio: Bowling Green State University Popular Press, 1997.

ROUDANE, MATTHEW C., ed. *The Cambridge Companion to Tennessee Williams.* Cambridge: Cambridge University Press, 1997.

SPOTO, DONALD. *The Kindness of Strangers: The Life of Tennessee Williams.* New York: Da Capo Press, 1997.

WILLIAMS, TENNESSEE. *Memoirs.* Garden City, New York: Doubleday, 1975.